Contents

Introduction

Welcome to Learn XPath Fast!

In this chapter, I'll answer some questions which you may have about XPath and about this book.

What is XPath?

XPath is a language for navigating the internal structure of XML data. It can also query XML data, to some extent.

Why should I learn it?

There are several reasons to learn XPath.

XPath lets you navigate and query XML. It lets you do this from a wide variety of other tools and programming languages. XPath is a web standard, so it's widely supported.

XPath lets you navigate and query Html. The structure of Html mirrors that of XML. XPath works on both and works in the same way, so XPath skills transfer between the two. Navigating Html is useful for tasks like creating automated tests for websites. XPath is supported by the Chrome browser and the widely-used testing tool, Selenium.

XPath helps you master other XML technologies. Other XML technologies, like XQuery and XSLT, are based around XPath, and they depend on it. XPath, on the other hand, works independently of them. It makes sense to learn XPath first.

Why should I buy this book?

It's practical

This book is about learning XPath as a skill. It explains language principles alongside examples and exercises, so you get practice applying what you learn, as you learn it.

It's convenient

No special software required

You only need Google Chrome. You won't have to install any other software. I'll show you how to run XPath directly in the browser, online or offline, so you can get started sooner.

No outside knowledge required

This book includes separate chapters to cover the XML you need.

No copying out long examples

The exercises require minimal typing. They are about using XPath to solve problems and building up your skill level in the process.

It's thorough

This book is designed to be suitable for beginners, but it's not just an introduction. It's designed as a course to study. It aims to give a thorough understanding of the language.

Its author is well-reviewed

If you're reading this book before it has any reviews, you can still find out what other readers think of my work. Take a look at books in my previous series "Learn Command Line and Batch Script Fast". It takes a similar exercise-based approach. It got good reviews.

Which version of XPath does this book cover?

This book covers the version that works with the widest range of tools and languages. Those include Chrome, Selenium, and Microsoft SQL Server (as part of XQuery). This book covers XPath 1.0.

Just as XQuery is based around XPath, other versions of XPath are based around version 1.0. What you learn in XPath 1.0 works in all versions of XPath, all versions of XQuery, and therefore, all the tools which support any of them.

Many applications, like Chrome and SQL Server, don't support other versions of XPath. XPath 1.0 does what they need. To use these tools, you have to use XPath 1.0.

What do you mean XPath works in SQL Server "as part of XQuery"?

SQL Server supports the use of XQuery to get data from XML stored in database tables.

XPath is a part of XQuery, among other things, and works in its place. This means you can also use XPath in SQL Server. You don't have to know XQuery to do this; just that valid XPath is also valid XQuery.

How best to use this book

It may help you to know a few things about this book in advance. I'll cover those here.

Book structure

The book has six sections:

1 - XML

2 - XPath Basics – using XPath and the Chrome console

3 - XPath Topics – in-depth coverage of each part of the language

4 - XML Namespaces

5 - XPath for working with namespaces

6 – Automatic XPath Generators – their uses and limits.

Why it's worth knowing

Sections 1 & 4 are included so that you can learn anything you need to about XML, within the book itself. They don't have any exercises which require access to a computer. They can be read straight through: on the bus, on the train, anywhere.

The other sections do have exercises. They require a computer with Google Chrome installed. They are also based on some sample XML and Html files, which you will need to copy or download. Once you have saved your own copies of the files, you won't need internet access to do the exercises.

XML namespaces do not apply to Html. If you are learning XPath so you can better automate website tests, you can safely skip sections 4 & 5.

Exercises

The exercises start out as instructions to follow, and quickly progress to problem-solving, as new concepts are introduced. This is to provide practice using new parts of the language and using different parts in combination.

All problem-solving exercises have an answer on the page after, for e-book readers, or at the end, for readers of the paperback version.

Contact

If you have any queries about this book or its contents, you can contact me at:

authordarmstrong@gmail.com

1 - XML

1.1 - Do I need to learn more about XML first?

If you've used XML or Html before, you probably know enough to *start* learning XPath right now.

This chapter covers what you need to know about XML to *finish* learning XPath from the rest of the book. It's here so that you can learn XPath without having to stop and look up, for example, what a processing-instruction node is. The only thing it won't cover is XML namespaces. There's a separate chapter for those later on.

1.2 - XML

XML stands for eXtensible Markup Language. It's a commonly used format for storing and exchanging data.

Below, I've put together some simplified examples of XML. I'll use them to introduce what it looks like and how it works, step by step.

Elements

Look at the example below.

```
<item>

    <product>eggs</product>

    <quantity>12</quantity>

    <price>1.99</price>

    <fragile />

</item>
```

This describes an "item" containing 12 eggs and costing $1.99 (we'll assume the currency is dollars). It notes that the item is fragile.

In the XML above, an example of an element is:

```
<product>eggs</product>
```

An element is typically made up of three parts:

An opening tag, e.g. "<product>"

A closing tag, e.g. "</product>"

Some content between the two, e.g. "eggs"

The tags "mark up" the content between them. That is, they label it in a way which allows both computers and humans to identify what that data is. The "eXtensible" in XML means that mark up language, like tag names, can be anything. It isn't pre-defined by the language designers. Whoever writes the XML document can make up whatever tags they like. If they want a "<monkey>" tag, they can have one.

An element can be much smaller, e.g. "<fragile />". This element has no content, so it consists of one tag which is marked closed by the "/" character.

An element can also be much larger and contain more than just text. In the example above, the "item" element encloses everything else. Its content includes other elements, and the content of those elements. This is called nesting. We can say that "product" is nested in "item".

Elements are the main building blocks of XML. The way they are nested inside each other is what gives XML its structure. Take the example below:

```
<item>

    <product>eggs</product>

    <quantity>12</quantity>

    <price>1.99</price>

    <fragile />

</item>

<item>

    <product>red onions</product>
```

```
    <quantity>3</quantity>

    <price>0.99</price>

  </item>
```

We can see that "fragile" is nested in the first item only, so eggs are fragile and onions are not. Likewise, we can see that there are three red onions and they cost $0.99, because all of that information is nested within the second item.

Text

In the example above, "red onions" is an example of text. However, "3" and "0.99" are also text, even though they are numeric values.

There is also text between element tags, e.g. between "<item>" and "<product>", or between "</product>" and "<quantity>". This is text consisting of spaces, tabs, new line characters, and so on. These characters cannot, by themselves, be seen, but they help create the layout for everything else. They are known as whitespace characters.

Attributes

Let's make the example a little more detailed. Look at the new version below.

```
  <item @id="100345">

    <product>eggs</product>

    <quantity>12</quantity>

    <price @currency="USD">1.99</price>

    <fragile />

  </item>
```

This describes an item containing 12 eggs and costing $1.99 in US Dollars (USD). It notes that the item is fragile. It gives the item an ID number of 100345.

We can tell the currency and the ID because they are recorded as attributes. In the attribute below:

@currency="USD"

We can see the syntax as follows:

@AttributeName="AttributeValue"

Attributes can be added to the opening tag of an element.

Comments

I'll use a different example of XML here. The XML below is the kind of thing you might see controlling routing within a network.

```
<ports>

    <port @id="COM01">OFF</port>

    <port @id="COM02">ON</port>

    <port @id="COM03">OFF</port>

    <!-- Only one COM port should be ON at a time -->

</ports>
```

A computer program might read this file and check which COM port was on, so it knows which port to send data to.

The "<!-- Only one COM port should be ON at a time -->" is a comment. It's there to be read by humans and ignored by the computer.

In this example, it's a note for IT support technicians. If they edit the file, to turn on a different COM port, for example, this reminds them to turn off any others at the same time.

Nodes

All of the above are types of node. Elements, text, attributes and comments are all nodes in XML.

These nodes form a structure known as a tree. It's a lot like a family tree. In the routing XML, for example, "ports" was the parent node, and each "port" element was a child node. The way nodes are nested within one another defines the relationships between them.

Look at the example below:

```
<shopping>

  <item>

    <product>red onions</product>

    <quantity>3</quantity>

    <price>0.99</price>

  </item>

</shopping>
```

Here, "quantity" is nested in "item". We can say that "quantity" is a child of "item". Likewise, "item" is the parent of "quantity".

The "product" and "price" nodes are also children of "item", so they are siblings of "quantity".

We can say that "price" is a descendant of "shopping" and that "shopping" is an ancestor of "price".

Note: children are also descendants, so "item" is a descendant of "shopping", as well as being its child. Likewise, parents are also ancestors.

Non-elements in the Node Tree

The non-element node types also fit into the node tree.

Text and comment nodes have no child nodes of their own, but they are children of the nodes they are nested in.

Attributes are not nested. They are not child nodes. Despite this, the element node they are declared in *is* their parent.

There are also some other types of node worth knowing about...

Root Node

An XML document is expected to have one element which contains all the others. That is, one element within which all the others are nested, directly or indirectly. This element is the ancestor of all other elements. It is known as the root element, or document element.

The root *node*, or document *node*, is something else. It is a node which is *not* written in the document. It exists in the logical structure of the node tree, as the parent of the root element. The root node represents the document itself. If you navigate an XML document using a tool like XPath, the root node is your starting point. It's where you navigate from.

Processing Instructions

These are like comments, except that they are not there for human readers. They are instructions for the application processing the XML. They may, for example, reference a stylesheet file, which says how to format the XML for on-screen display: e.g. element tags in blue, text in black, etc.

Processing instructions follow the format:

<?Some text?>

Namespaces

XML also has namespace nodes, but we'll deal with namespaces later.

2 - XPath Basics

2.1 – How to use the sample files

Get the sample files:
Go to https://github.com/Author-D-Armstrong/XPath

On the web page, click the green "Clone or download" button, and choose the "Download ZIP" option.

Once the ZIP file has downloaded, and appears in the bottom bar of the browser, click on it and choose "Show in folder".

Right click on the file and choose "Extract All". This will create a normal folder, containing all the files.

Note
GitHub also lets you open the files directly online. However, if you do that, it reformats them and then XPaths don't work on them anymore.

Open the sample files in Chrome (in Windows 10):
First, make sure the machine you are using has Chrome installed! If not, download it from Google and install it.

Right-click on one of the XML files you have downloaded.

Select "Open With" then choose Chrome if it's listed or "Choose Another App" if not.

Select "More Apps", then "Look for another app on this PC". This opens the File Explorer.

Typically, Chrome will be in the C: drive, e.g. C:\Program Files (x86)\Google\Chrome\Application

Choose "chrome". The file should open in Google Chrome.

Make XML files open in Chrome automatically:
Right-click on one of the XML files you have downloaded.

Select "Open With" then "Choose Another App".

Now that you have used Chrome to open an XML file, it will appear in the app list.

Make sure Chrome is selected. Tick the box "Always use this app to open XML files". Click "OK".

The file will open in Chrome.

More importantly, whenever you open any XML file from now on, it will open in Chrome by default.

The Html file may open in Chrome by default already, but if not, you can repeat the process above with that too.

2.2 - How to run XPath in Chrome

Exercise 1: ready the console
Open Google Chrome!

Right-click on your homepage.

A context menu will appear.

On the menu, click on "Inspect".

A panel will open in your browser. At the top of the panel, you will see several tabs.

Click on the one titled "Console".

The contents of this tab may be blank, or may contain some text already.

If your console contains text, click on the icon of the circle with a diagonal line through it. This will clear the console.

The console should contain a cursor, blinking on and off. If it doesn't, just click inside the console and the cursor will appear.

Exercise 2: run a test XPath
Firstly, we need to make sure that you can run an XPath at all.

Type:

$x('1+1')

Press return.

You should see the number two appear.

Success!

You just ran an XPath expression in Chrome and it worked.

Explanation

The Chrome console lets you enter and run JavaScript against a webpage or file which is open in your browser.

The function - $x() – is an extension of JavaScript, built-into Chrome. It allows you to run XPath expressions against an open web page or XML document, from the console.

The function requires an XPath expression, formatted as a text string. Our XPath expression was "1+1". To make it a string, we used quotation marks, " ' ", at each end. We used single-quotes, but double-quotes would also work.

Exercise 3: explore an XML file

The XML file used in this chapter is fairly complex. It has several levels of nesting and a variety of node types at each. It lets us explore many key features of XPath in one place.

To make the document structure easier to grasp, I'll introduce its main features here first. See below.

This XML document is a list of learning resources - books, videos, etc - for various IT skills. The resources are all children of the root element: index.

```
<index>

    <book></book>

    <video></video>

    <book></book>

</index>
```

However, unlike in the XML above, within each resource element is nested information about that resource: its author, title, and so on.

```
<book>

    <author>D Armstrong</author>

    <title>Learn XPath Fast</title>

</book>
```

Some resources also have a "metadata" element containing a list of relevant keywords.

```
<book>

    <title>Learn XPath Fast</title>

    <metadata>

        <keyword>XPath</keyword>

        <keyword>XML</keyword>

    </metadata>

</book>
```

Some of the elements have attributes.

```
<book id="eb1" lang="English">
```

There are a few comments too.

```
<!-- What a great book! -->
```

That's all.

Open "Resources.xml".

Have a look around the document before moving on. Try clicking the triangle symbols by the elements' opening tags. These collapse and expand elements, hiding or showing their descendants. If you want to focus on just one resource, for example, you can collapse the others.

Exercise 4: run an XPath on XML

Run the XPath:

    $x('//index')

Note: XPath is case-sensitive. If you use, for example, "Index" (with a capital "I"), in your expression, then it won't find any matches in this document.

You should see the "index" node appear in the console, inside square brackets, with a triangle symbol next to it.

Click on the symbol to open an expanded view of the node and its contents. Some of the contents will themselves be expandable.

Exercise 5: explore your results in the Chrome Console

Expand "0: index" to see the index node's properties and their values.

Find the children property.

This will expand to show the books, video, etc, which are child nodes of the index node. These will match what you see in the XML document itself.

You could expand the child nodes too, if you wanted, in the same way. You could expand a book, then its children property, then the title, and look up the inner Html property to see the title text.

You won't normally need to do all of that. Often, when you run an XPath, you will see, right away, whether or not it returned the nodes you intended. However, if your XPath returned one of several similar-looking nodes, such as, in this document, a keyword node, you might want to expand it to look at its text, or another property, and check you got the right node.

Explanation: how the XPath worked

Inside the "$x()" function, you used this XPath:

//index

The function searches the XML document's node tree. It starts at the root node, i.e. the document, and navigates from there, according to the XPath expression you entered. The expression we used has two parts. Here's the breakdown of what they mean.

Part one, "//", means "this node's descendants..."

Using "//" at the beginning of an XPath means "the root node's descendants", i.e. search the whole document.

Part two, "index", means "...of the type: index".

In summary, the XPath searches the whole document for element nodes of the type "index" and returns any it finds as a set of nodes, or "node set".

In this case, there is only one "index" node, so there is only one item in the set. It is still a set though.

Although words like "index" and "metadata" may sound technical, they have no special meaning in XML. They could just as easily be "resource_list" and "keyword_list".

You can identify words which *do* have special meanings in XML by the fact that they are prefixed with "xml". An example would be "xmlns", or XML NameSpace, which we'll cover towards the end of the book.

Exercise 6: retrieve XML

OK, that's enough information to write your own XPath.

In the console, write the XPath expression to retrieve all the book nodes from the document.

Run it and see if it works.

Then turn to the next page (on e-reader) or the back of the book (in the paperback) to see the answer.

Note for readers of the paperback version: it's important to check the back of the book after each exercise, even if you can see that your answer worked. There are often additional notes, or alternative answers, included with an answer. That material is "part of the course", and some of it is essential to understanding what comes after the exercise.

Exercise 7: check for absent nodes

Run:

```
$x('//magazine')
```

See what it returns.

Make sure the cursor is still in the console. Then press the UP key.

The last XPath expression you ran should appear at the prompt, in an editable form.

Press the UP key again.

The XPath before that should appear.

Exercise 9: use a simple filter
Run:

```
$x('//book[position() = 3]')
```

This will return only one book node. It returns the node at position three in the set of book nodes.

Now use XPath to get the first node in the set.

2.3 - How to navigate using XPath

XPath lets you search a whole document and filter your results in many ways.

Often though, you don't need to search the whole document. Often, you just need to search part of it, e.g. nodes nested within a particular element. On my example webpage, doing this lets you answer questions like:

What is the title of the video?

Which book titles are listed?

What is the last book's title? What is its ID?

Which resource is part of a series?

XPath navigation lets you find answers to all of the above. The examples in this chapter will show how. In doing so, they introduce the basics of XPath navigation.

To keep the example code clear, from now on, only the XPath part will be shown, like this:

//video

You will still need to use the "$x()" function and quotation marks in the console.

Example: what is the title of the video?
Start by running the XPath:

//video/title

The meaning of this expression can be broken down to:

//video

Find any "video"node(s)...

/

...then find their/its child node(s)...

title

...of type "title"

This returns the title node. If you want to see the text, expand the node and look at the "innerHtml" property. You should see "Installing Selenium in Visual Studio".

It is also possible to make XPath return a node's text directly, but we'll cover that later in the book.

This example demonstrates three new concepts. I'll cover each of them, with exercises, below.

Concept 1 - Context nodes:

Once part of an XPath finds a node, that node becomes the "context node". The context node is where the rest of the XPath expression starts searching from. Once the XPath finds the video node, the video becomes the context node.

That's why "/title" starts searching from the video node. It's why it only matches the title element nested within the video element.

Exercise 10: navigate to child nodes

Write a new XPath. Get the three video keyword nodes.

Exercise 11: navigate child nodes with predicates - 1

Get the second keyword of the first book.

Get the first keyword of the second book.

Concept 2 - Axes:

A graph has x and y axes and each runs in two directions: positive and negative. XPath has axes relating to its node-tree structure and each runs in only one direction.

In the example, we used the child axis to navigate from the video to the title:

    //video/title

The child axis is the default axis, so there's no need to write it in the XPath, but if you did, it would be:

    //video/child::title

For comparison, if you wanted to find the node containing the video, i.e. video's parent node, you could do this:

    //video/parent::index

This example is a bit contrived, but we'll put the parent axis to better use later in the chapter.

There are many more axes. We'll cover them in full later in the book.

Concept 3 - Node tests:

The node type names, like video, title, and index, act as node tests. That is, they test node type and only return nodes of a matching type.

You may want to return nodes regardless of their type. For example, maybe you want the video's parent node, whatever type of node it is. In that case, you could do this:

//video/parent::node()

The "node()" is also a node test, except it matches and returns any node, whatever type it is. In this case, the index element is the node on the parent axis, so "node()" returns that.

Only element nodes and the root node can be parents. Using "node()" will work in either case.

If we are sure the parent node will be an element, we can do this:

//video/parent::*

The "*" symbol, known as "glob", matches any element node.

It ignores other nodes, like text nodes, comments, and the root node.

Exercise 13: use a node test
Get all the child nodes of the video.

Exercise 14: use another node test
Get all the resources, whatever type they are (book, video, etc).

Exercise 15: use an axis
Get the resource(s) with a narrator.

Example: which book titles are listed?
Run:

//book/title

This returns child title nodes of any book nodes in the document. XPath applies "/title" to each node found by "//book".

Run:

> //book[position() = last()]/title

The "last()" function returns the number of nodes in a node set. This number is known as the context size. You can use it to get the last node in a set, as above.

Exercise 16: use defaults, save typing
The last function returns a number. Knowing that, can you shorten the XPath above?

Example: what is the ID of the last book?
The book ID is an attribute node. You can't navigate to it in the same way as you did to the title node. It isn't on the child axis. Instead, you would use the attribute axis:

> //book[last()]/attribute::id

That's a lot of typing though, so here's the shorthand version:

> //book[last()]/@id

The "@" is shorthand for "attribute::".

If we wanted any and all attributes of the last book, not just the ID, we would run:

> //book[last()]/@*

When used with "@", the "*" will match any attribute-type nodes.

Exercise 17: navigate to an attribute node
Get the language attribute of the last book.

Exercise 18: navigate to the attributes of a node set - 1
Get the language attributes of all books.

Exercise 19: navigate to the attributes of a node set - 2
Get the language attributes of all resources.

Exercise 20: navigate to the attributes of a node set - 3
Get all attributes in the document.

Note: you will get (many) more results than you expect. I'll explain why after the answer.

Chrome XML formatting
Due to the way Chrome displays XPath in the browser, i.e. using Html to format it, there are lots of attributes that you can't see which are still present on the page.

XPath can query Html, just as it does XML, so it returns all the attributes from both.

This is the downside of using Chrome to test XPath expressions. However, you can usually avoid this problem by navigating to an XML node at the beginning of your XPath. For example:

//index//@*

That way, you get the XML root element, e.g. "index", and then only get the attributes within that, i.e. all the XML attributes.

Outside of XML documents opened in Chrome, this isn't usually an issue.

When using XPath to query a web page, e.g. for browser test automation, there is normally only Html present.

When using XPath to query XML, e.g. in SQL Server, there is normally only XML present.

In those cases, you can use "/" to start navigating from the root node of the document, which is more efficient. We'll cover how to do that later, in the chapter on using XPath in Html.

Exercise 21: navigate to an attribute by position
Get the last attribute of the video.

Example: which resource is part of a series?
By now, you have covered enough XPath to get the answer yourself. Exercise time!

Exercise 22: problem solving
Find out which resource is part of a series.

Exercise 23: use an axis faster
Find out which type of resource has a narrator. This time use the shorthand.

More on shorthand
Many of the most commonly-used features of XPath have shorthand versions.

One such shorthand is what you just used to search the whole document for narrator nodes. It is:

```
//
```

This is shorthand for:

/descendant-or-self::node()/

We use "//" followed by a node test, as in:

//narrator

This gets you the descendants of the root node. However, it gets them on the child axes of their parent nodes, rather than on any descendant axes. To see why, we need to look at the longhand version.

/descendant-or-self::node()/child::narrator

The child axis is used simply because it is the default axis.

How "//" works

Starting from the root node, the "descendant-or-self" axis returns all of the root node's descendants, i.e. anything nested within it, directly or indirectly. It also returns the root node itself.

It returns them to the node test "node()" which matches all node types: root node, elements, text nodes, etc.

XPath then navigates the child axis for each of these. As only the root and element nodes can have children, the axis returns only:

children of the root node

children of the root node's descendant elements

Taken together, these are all the descendants of the root node.

The final node test then returns only the narrator node(s).

Using "//" elsewhere

You can also use "//" in the middle of an XPath:

//book//keyword

This returns all the book keywords. That is, all the keyword elements which are descendants of book elements.

Syntax

XPath navigation expressions follow a simple syntax:

/axis::nodetest[predicate]

The predicate is optional. The shorthand and defaults can sometimes hide the syntax, but it is always there.

Example:

//book[1]

This is shorthand for:

/descendant-or-self::node()/child::book[position() = 1]

This expression actually navigates twice, so let's break it down:

/descendant-or-self::node()

/child::book[position() = 1]

Each part follows the syntax:

/axis::nodetest[predicate]

We can repeat the pattern as many times as necessary.

2.4 - Recap

We have covered a lot already:

Commonly-used axes and associated shorthand
child:

    no shorthand

        (it's the default axis)

parent:

    ..

        short for: parent::node()

attribute:

    @

        short for: attribute::

descendant-or-self:

    //

        short for: /descendant-or-self::node()/

Node Tests
Match any node: node()

Match any element node: *

Predicates
Filter by position: e.g. [1]

Functions
Context Position : position()

Context Size: last()

Tools and techniques

How to run XPath in Chrome

How to use the Chrome console efficiently

Basic syntax

/axis::nodetest[predicate]

Other Concepts

Root node

Context node

Context size

Context position

3 – XPath Topics

3.1 - Node Tests

Node tests are an essential component of XPath expressions.

What are node tests?

Node tests are the part of XPath which filters nodes by type.

Any node name can act as a test. If you want to get all the book nodes in a document, you might write:

```
//book
```

In the above, "book" is a node test.

More generic node tests

There are other node tests though. This chapter is about those: the node tests universal to all XML documents.

They are:

```
* (glob)
```

any element node

```
node()
```

any node, e.g. element, comment, text

```
comment()
```

comment nodes

```
text()
```

text nodes - these often contain only whitespace

```
processing-instruction()
```

processing instruction nodes

The attribute axis

You can use node tests with the attribute axis, i.e.

@*

@node()

Using "@*" selects attributes.

Using "@node()" selects attributes and namespace nodes.

Practice Exercises

Exercise 24: use processing-instruction()

Find any processing instructions within the document.

Note: although the XML document declaration at the top of the page has the same format as a processing instruction, it isn't one, so won't be returned.

Exercise 25: use node()

Get all the child *nodes* of video.

Exercise 26: use glob

Get all the child *elements* of video.

Exercise 27: get a comment node

Get the comment node from video

Exercise 28: get the text node from an element

Get the text node for the video's title.

Exercise 29: understand the text nodes among an element's children

Get the text nodes from video. Expand them to see what their text is.

Text vs. Text Nodes

A text node, as returned by "text()", is not just a string. It is part of the node tree. You can navigate onwards from a text node, to its parent node, for example. You can't navigate anywhere from just a text string.

You can, however, use XPath to return just a text string and not the node which contains it. We'll cover that later, in the chapter on data type functions.

3.2 - Predicates

What predicates are

A predicate is a condition against which nodes in a set can be judged. It returns a value of either true or false for each node. If it returns true for a node, that node is returned by the XPath expression using the predicate.

For example, in:

//index/*[position() = 3]

The predicate is:

position() = 3

The predicate is only true for the third child element of index, so only that node is returned.

However, predicates are not limited to node positions or even to dealing with nodes. A predicate can be any expression that returns true or false.

A trivial example:

//book[1=1]

//book[1=0]

The top example always returns all the book nodes, because one is always equal to one. The second example always returns an empty set, because one is never equal to zero.

To make a predicate useful though, we need to make it depend on the context node in some way.

How navigation affects predicates

Before you move on to using new types of predicate, you should understand how they will be applied to the XML node tree.

Take this example:

    //book

This returns all the books.

Now try:

    //book[1]

This returns the first book: so far, so good.

If we want to get the keywords from all the books, we can do this:

    //book/metadata/keyword

This returns all the keywords.

Exercise 30: prediction

Suppose you want to get the first keyword. Will the XPath below work?

    //book/metadata/keyword[1]

To understand why this happens, look at how the XML node tree is structured.

In this case:

    book 1

        metadata

            keyword 1

keyword 2

keyword 3

book 2

  metadata

    keyword 1

    keyword 2

    keyword 3

etc

Look at the XPath again:

//book/metadata/keyword[1]

The predicate "[1]" makes the XPath get each keyword which is first in its own context, i.e. the child axis of the metadata for a book. This means the predicate is true for the first keyword *in each book*, so that is what the XPath returns.

That's why you get multiple nodes. XPath deals with each "metadata" context separately, so there can be multiple first nodes.

Likewise, if you run:

//keyword[1]

You still get multiple nodes. The keywords are still being accessed via the child axes of their parent elements.

Whereas, if you run:

//book[1]

This returns only one node, because all the books are children of the same parent.

Exercise 31: use predicates better
Change the XPath below, so that it does return only the first keyword from the whole set of books.

   //book/metadata/keyword[1]

Exercise 32: save some typing
Write a shorter XPath that gets the same result.

   Hint: //

How predicates affect navigation
You can keep navigating after using a predicate.

For example:

   //index/*[3]/title

This gets you the title of the third resource.

The three ways to use predicates
There are three things a predicate can use to filter nodes. They are:

   Numbers

   Boolean values (true or false)

   Node sets

We've already covered numbers. Any expression which is, or returns, a number can be used as a predicate, and XPath will automatically compare it to the node's context position, returning a Boolean value to filter the node against.

Often, you will need to filter nodes by condition like "is the price of the book below $10?" You can do this by using expressions which return Boolean values. I'll show how shortly.

To be useful though, those Boolean expressions usually have to be based on node sets. For example, in the above, they would be based on the set of price nodes in the book. Therefore, to use these expressions properly, you need to understand how predicates use node sets, so we'll cover that first.

Using node sets in predicates

How can you use node sets in predicates?

Why would you want to?

Let's take some examples:

    //index/*[narrator]

This returns any resource which has a narrator (as a child element).

We aren't limited to child elements though. We can use the full XPath syntax inside a predicate, axes, node tests, everything.

For example:

    //index/*[metadata/keyword]

This returns any resource which has a keyword (in its metadata).

When you use an XPath expression within a predicate, it starts navigating from the predicate's context node, in this case, whatever the "* matched. It uses the child axis, by default. It returns a node set, into the predicate, and that node set gets converted to a Boolean.

Empty node sets are converted to false. Non-empty node sets are converted to true.

That's how the expressions above work. For example, searching for a narrator only returns nodes when starting from the audiobook node. Starting from any other resource, the search returns an empty set. Therefore, the predicate returns true only for the non-empty set, so the XPath using it returns only the audiobook node.

Exercise 33: use a node set in a predicate
Get any resource which has a url (as a child node)

Exercise 34: use a node set in a predicate
Get any resource which has a comment (as a child node)

Navigation inside predicates
You can also use axes inside predicates, longhand or shorthand:

    //index/*[attribute::*]

    //index/*[@*]

These return any child elements of index which have one or more attributes.

Exercise 35: use an axis in a predicate
Get any resources which have id attributes.

Exercise 36: use an axis in a predicate - 2
Get any element with a language attribute ("lang").

Using Booleans in predicates

As shown earlier, any expression that returns a Boolean can be used as a predicate. However, usually, we will want the expression to use values from within nodes.

Using a node's child elements in predicates

A predicate can refer to a value within a node's children.

Example:

    //book[price < 10]

This gets all the books with a price less than $10.

What if the resource doesn't have a price node?

The video, for example, is free online. It doesn't have a price node.

Exercise 37: prediction

Don't run the XPath below yet. What do you think it would return?

    //video[price < 10]

Of course, elements may have multiple child nodes:

    //book[metadata/keyword = "Cmd Line"]

This gets any book which has at least one keyword with the string value: "Cmd Line".

If a node set is used in a Boolean expression, then the expression tests whether any of the nodes return true. That's why only one keyword has to match, for the book to be returned.

Exercise 38: check values of child elements

Get any book with a price above $10

Exercise 39: check child elements for a value

Get any resource with a keyword of "Selenium".

Using other axes

A predicate can also refer to a value via other axes, not just "child". It can, for example, use the attribute axis. Try out the following:

    //book[@id = "eb1"]

Exercise 40: use attribute values in predicates

Get any resource with a language of "English".

Exercise 41: navigate on

Get the titles of those resources (where they do have titles).

Using a node's value in predicates

Earlier, we used a predicate to get books with prices below $10. But suppose we wanted to just get book prices below $10, i.e. the price nodes themselves. Can you do it?

Exercise 42: get the nodes you filter on

For books, get price nodes with values less than $10.

Exercise 43: try out the self axis

Run:

    //book/price/.

Run:

//book/price

What's the difference in the results?

Exercise 44: use self in a predicate
Get any price nodes below $5, whether for books or not.

3.3 - Nesting predicates

You can use XPath navigation expressions within predicates. Can you use predicates in these expressions, i.e. within other predicates? Yes, you can.

Example:

//book[metadata/keyword[2] = "XML"]

This gets any book with "XML" as the second keyword. We can say that the predicate "[2]" is nested in the other predicate.

Exercise 45: use nested predicates - 1
Get all the resources which have keywords.

You won't have to use nesting here. This exercise is just a set-up for the next one.

Exercise 46: use nested predicates - 2
Get the resource, of any type, where the last keyword is "Testing".

Exercise 47: use nested predicates - 3
Change your last XPath to get only the resources with at least three keywords.

3.4 - Functions

A function is something which returns a value. The value might be a number, a text string, or a Boolean. It depends on which function you use.

You have already used some functions: position and last. They returned numbers for use in predicate expressions. Functions can do much more than that though.

Over the course of this book, I'll introduce the other XPath functions. I'll explain how they work. I'll provide scenarios where you can use them.

There are a lot of functions though, so I'll cover them one group at a time, between the other chapters.

The specification for XPath 1.0 groups functions by data type. That makes four groups:

Boolean

number

string

node set

I'll group functions a little differently. Some of them convert between data types. These functions have a lot in common. I'll introduce them as a separate group:

data type functions.

Also, some of the node set functions relate to XML namespaces, which won't be covered until later in the book. I'll introduce those functions then, after covering how XML namespaces work.

3.5 - Boolean Functions

The Boolean functions are:

true

false

not

lang

It may seem strange that "lang" is classified as a Boolean function, but it does return a Boolean value.

Functions: true and false

XPath makes use of the Boolean values, true and false. However, if you try to use the words "true" or "false" as Boolean values in an XPath expression, you get an error. For example, try to run the following:

true

It doesn't work. It isn't recognised as a Boolean. However, you can use the function:

true()

This will return the Boolean value:

true

That value can then be used by the XPath expression.

Likewise, you can use "false()" instead of "false".

We'll use these functions when we cover Boolean operators, and when we cover the "not" function, next.

Run this:

    not(true())

You should get:

    false

If you run:

    not(false())

You get:

    true

The "not" function takes a Boolean value as input and outputs the opposite: true for false and false for true.

Many functions have inputs, or "arguments". Arguments are written inside the brackets following a function.

The arguments can be values, or expressions which return values. For example:

    not(1=2)

The "1=2" returns false. It returns it into the "not" function, as an argument, and the function returns the opposite: true.

You can use the function in predicates, as in the XPath below:

    //book[not(position() = 1)]

This gets all books except the first one.

Exercise 48: use not

Get all books except the last.

Multiple arguments

If a function takes more than one argument, they are separated by commas, like so:

    function(argument1,argument2)

Checking for non-existence

In the predicates chapter, we used predicates to check if nodes existed.

For example:

    //index/*[url]

This went to the index node and returned any of its child elements which had URLs.

A predicate expects a Boolean input. If you give a node set to something which expects a Boolean, the node set gets converted to a Boolean, which is then used.

The "not" function also expects a Boolean input, but you can give it a node set. Knowing that, can you solve the exercises below?

Exercise 49: check nodes don't exist

Can you work out how to get the child nodes which don't have URLs?

Exercise 50: check certain types of nodes don't exist

Get any resources which don't have a price.

Get any resources which don't have a price above $10.

Function: lang

For this function, visit my web page and open up the "languages" XML file.

Example

Run:

    //title[lang("en")]

You will get the nodes for the two English versions of the title.

This function returns a Boolean. It returns true for any XPath node which has an "xml:lang" attribute that matches the one specified, in this case "en" for English.

As the type of English is not specified, the function matches any and all English language title nodes. US and GB English are both included.

Example: upper case

Run:

    //title[lang("EN")]

You will get the same result as before. This shows that, unlike most of XPath, this function is not case-sensitive.

Exercise 52: get a specific dialect

Can you guess how to get only the title nodes which are American English? Try it.

Exercise 53: see how language attributes are applied to XML

Use XPath to search for all elements with a language of English.

Note: you may find more than you expect.

Exercise 54: avoid a specific dialect

Return nodes for any titles which are not in English.

Xml:lang vs. other language attributes

If you ran this function on the "resources.xml" document, it wouldn't do anything. The attributes there are only "lang" not "xml:lang", so the function ignores them.

The "lang" attributes in the resources document are normal XML attribute names. If they were renamed "language", they would work just the same way. In the resources document, they refer to the languages of those resources.

The "xml:lang" attribute is different. It is a reserved attribute.

All attributes which begin with "xml" are reserved. That is, they have a specific purpose defined by the creators of XML.

In this case, that purpose is to identify the language(s) of the text used in the XML file itself, e.g. the text content of the title nodes. That's why the "lang" function works with "xml:lang", and not with anything else.

3.6 - Operators

The XPath operators fall into five groups:

Comparison

Arithmetic

Node set

Logical

Navigation

Comparison operators

There are six comparison operators:

=

    equal to

!=

    not equal to

>

    greater than

<

    less than

>=

    greater than or equal to

<=

    less than or equal to

It's easy to test out what they do. Here are some test expressions and their results.

Equal to:

    1 = 1

        true

    1 = 2

        false

Not equal to:

    1 != 1

        false

    1 != 2

        true

Greater than:

    1 > 2

        false

Less than:

    1 < 2

        true

You can also compare text strings:

    "cat" = "mouse"

        false

"cat" != "mouse"

true

Note the following though:

"cats" = "CATS"

false

The string comparison is case-sensitive.

Using the comparison operators: predicates

Earlier, we used shorthand such as:

//book[2]

This returns the second book in the document.

The longhand version is:

//book[position() = 2]

It does the same thing, so it may seem unnecessary. However, you can also do things like this:

//book[position() != 2]

This gets you all the other books in the document: all except the second. You can't do that with the shorthand version.

We can also do this:

//book[position() > 2]

This returns all the books after the first two.

Exercise 55: use comparison operators

Get the first two books.

Exercise 56: use comparison operators - 2

Earlier, we used the "last()" function to get the position of the last node. Can you get all the nodes except the last one?

Comparison operators are not limited to filtering nodes by their position. That's just a convenient example to show how they work. They can be used to filter on node content as well, which is much more useful. In fact, you already did this in the predicates chapter, e.g.

//book[price > 10]

This returns all the books with a price above $10.

Exercise 57: use comparison operators - 3

Get the free books, if there are any.

Exercise 58: use comparison operators - 4

Get any resources which have no price or which have a price of zero.

Arithmetic Operators

There are five arithmetic operators:

+

plus

-

minus

*

    star (multiplication)

div

    divide by

mod

    modulus (remainder of a division)

These are also simple to try out. Run the following XPath expressions:

    2 + 2

    5 - 10

    99 * 101

    52 div 10

The results show that XPath supports negative numbers and decimals.

We didn't try the "mod" operator yet:

    52 mod 10

This returns the remainder: two. That is, ten goes into fifty-two five times, and two is left over.

You may use "mod" with two numbers which divide perfectly, for example:

    4 mod 2

There is no remainder here, so this returns zero.

Uses

You can use all of these operators on node values. You can use them to return a number to the console, or into a predicate expression.

For example:

> //book[1]/price + //book[2]/price

This gets the combined price of the first two books.

Exercise 59: use math

Suppose you have a $2.50 e-book coupon. Get the remaining cost of buying the first book.

Exercise 60: use math to filter - 1

Get the second last book in the document.

Exercise 61: use math to filter - 2

Suppose there is a half price sale on all these resources. Get the books which will be under $10.

Exercise 62: use math to filter - 3

Get every other book in the document: the ones with even-numbered context positions, i.e. the second book, the fourth book, etc.

Brackets

We can also use:

> ()

brackets

These are precedence, rather than arithmetic, operators. They control the order of operations. Operations in brackets happen first, or "take precedence". For example:

(1 + 2) * 3

This becomes:

3 * 3

Then:

9

Whereas with:

1 + (2 * 3)

This becomes:

1 + 6

Then:

7

Infinity
If you run this:

7 div 0

It returns infinity. Some programming languages can't handle infinity and so will report an error if you try to divide by zero. XPath can handle infinity, so doesn't error. You can even go on to re-use the value, for example:

(7 div 0) > 3

This returns true.

Also, if you run this:

-7 div 0

You will see that XPath also supports negative infinity

This means you will never get a divide-by-zero error in XPath.

Node Set Operators

There are two of these:

|

union

()

brackets (flatten node sets)

Union

The union operator combines node sets.

Example 1

//video | //audiobook

This XPath returns the video and audiobook nodes, as one set.

Example 2

//book[1] | //index/*[1]

This returns the first book element and the first child element of resources. These are the same element, so the resulting set contains only one node. Union doesn't return duplicate nodes.

Example 3

//book[1]/metadata/keyword | //book[2]/metadata/keyword

This returns all of the keyword elements, even though some of those elements look identical. Union doesn't de-duplicate nodes by their type or text content, but by *where* they are from in the node tree.

Example 4

//keyword | //author

This returns all keywords and authors. You can combine any two node sets; they don't have to be children of the same parent, or of similar type. You can union attribute and element nodes if you want to.

Exercise 63: combine node sets - 1

Get, as a set, all the nodes which refer to people: author, presenter and narrator.

Exercise 64: combine node sets - 2

Get all the comment and processing instruction nodes.

A note on node sets

You might have noticed that node sets never contain duplicate nodes, i.e. multiple copies of a node from the same place in the XML document. In computing, a set is, by definition, a collection without duplicates. If two parts of any XPath, whether or not it uses the union operator, return the same node, the node is only added to the results once.

Brackets and node sets

Earlier, brackets were introduced as precedence operators. They were used to control the order of other operations in a calculation.

Brackets can also be used with node sets.

Example:

　//book/metadata/keyword[1]

This returns the first keyword from each book.

　(//book/metadata/keyword)[1]

This returns the first keyword from all the book keywords.

In the first example, each book has a set of keywords, and the predicate is applied to each keyword within the context of that book's metadata.

In the second example, the brackets tell XPath to combine the keyword node sets first. The predicate is applied to the resulting set afterwards.

The brackets are still acting as a precedence operator here. They return, to the rest of the XPath, what you would have seen returned to the console window, had you run:

　//book/metadata/keyword

They just allow you to re-use the result.

Exercise 65: re-use node sets - 1
Get the last keyword from all the book keywords.

Exercise 66: re-use node sets - 2
Get the last XML element in the document.

Exercise 67: re-use node sets - 3
Get the combined keywords of the video, audiobook and website nodes. Use "keyword" only once in your XPath expression.

Logical operators:

There are two of these:

and

logical AND

or

logical OR

Earlier, we showed that comparison operators return values of true or false. The logical operators do the same. The "and" operator returns true only if the values on each side of it are true.

Example:

(1=1) and (2=2)

Both of the above comparisons return true, so the "and" operator returns true as well.

Whereas:

(1=1) and (2=3)

If either condition returns false, the "and" operator returns false too, as it does here.

The "or" operator, on the other hand, returns true if either, or both, of the values it sits between are true.

true() or true()

true

true() or false()

true

false() or true()

true

false() or false()

false

It only returns false if neither condition is met.

Logical operators in use

These operators allow you to combine multiple criteria into one.

Examples: ranges

We can use "and" to filter by a value range:

//book[price >= 1 and price <= 100]

This returns all the books with prices from $1 to $100.

We can use "or" in a similar way:

//book[price < 1or price > 100]

This returns all of the books outside of that price range.

Examples: unrelated criteria

The criteria don't have to use the same field:

//book[position() <= 3 and price < 10]

This returns:

any books in positions one to three, priced below $10.

Whereas:

//book[position() <= 3 or price < 10]

This returns:

any books in positions one to three, and...

any books priced below $10.

Exercise 68: multiple conditions - 1

Check for books with a format of "Paperback" and a price over $10.

Exercise 69: multiple conditions - 2

Check for any books in an e-book format. Make sure you get them all.

Remember that XPath is case-sensitive, so "Ebook" won't match "ebook", for example.

Navigation operators

This is really just a term used to refer to shorthand like "//". Those are covered elsewhere, so I won't repeat them here.

3.7 - Chaining predicates

You can use a predicates in a chain, i.e. several different predicates, one after the other. This lets you filter node sets repeatedly.

For example, if we start with a single-predicate XPath:

//book[format != "Paperback"]

The "!=" operator used above checks if two values are different, and returns true if so. This gets any books which are NOT in a paperback format, i.e. all the e-books.

If we chain another predicate to the end:

//book[format != "Paperback"][3]

This gets the third of those e-books.

Exercise 70: chaining - 1
Find the first book, if any, with a price above $10

Exercise 71: chaining - 2
Return the first book, but only if it has a price above $10. Otherwise return an empty node set.

Exercise 72: chaining - 3
Return any books priced under $10 with the author "D Armstrong".

Chaining vs. the "and" operator
The logical operator "and" can be used in predicates.

Example:

//keyword[position() = 2 and position() = last()]

This checks for any keyword which is both the second and the last one listed for that same resource.

Only one resource (the website) has exactly two keywords, so only one keyword is returned: the second keyword for that resource.

The "and" operator lets you check both conditions are true. It combines those conditions into one predicate, against which each node is tested.

This is not the same as chaining.

Example:

//keyword[2][last()]

This returns all the keywords which are listed second for their resource.

Why does this happen?

Chaining works differently to "and". If you break the expression down, it works as follows:

//keyword

Part one returns all the keywords from all the resources, i.e. several groups of keywords, although they appear as a single list in the console.

//keyword[2]

Part two returns each keyword which is second in each of those groups, i.e. second in its own context. Effectively, it returns several groups, each containing one keyword node. Again, this is shown as a single list in the console.

//keyword[2][last()]

Part three returns each node which is last in those groups. As those groups now only contain one node each, every node remaining is last in its group and is returned.

Chaining vs. the "and" operator – part 2

The "and" operator and chaining may sometimes produce the same end result.

Example:

//book[price < 10 and author = "D Armstrong"]

This produces the same result as:

//book[price < 10][author = "D Armstrong"]

Side note: quotation marks

In this book, I use double-quotes around text strings, and single quotes around the whole XPath. It also works the other way round, for example:

$x("//book[author = 'D Armstrong']")

3.8 - Data Type Functions

XPath has four data types: node set, string, number and Boolean.

Each data type, apart from node set, has a function which converts to that type. These functions are named after the type they convert to. For example, the function "string" converts a number, Boolean, or node set, to a string.

These functions matter because XPath uses them, whether you tell it to or not.

When you provide one data type to something which expects another, e.g. a node set into a predicate or a number into the "not" function, XPath converts it. It converts it to the expected data type, using these functions, internally. That means the functions define how type conversion works in XPath.

Understanding these functions is essential to understanding how XPath works.

Function: string

Let's use examples to see the features of the string function.

Example: use the string function on a number
Run:

    string(1)

You should see:

    "1"

The quotation marks indicate that the number has been converted to text.

Example: use the string function on a Boolean
Run:

1=1

This will return the Boolean value:

true

Now run:

string(1=1)

You should see:

"true"

Note the quotation marks. The value has been converted to text.

Finally, run:

string(1=0)

You should see:

"false"

Example: use the string function on a node set
Run:

string(//book/title)

You should see only the first book title in the document.

You gave the function a whole node set containing multiple title nodes. What happened to all the other nodes and their text?

Answer: the function ignored them. It returns the text of the first node only.

Exercise 73: get the text content of a comment
Get the text from the first comment of the document.

If you run:

string(//book)

What do you expect to see? Run it and find out if you're right.

Get the text for all the resources in the document.

Example: use the string function in a predicate

Run:

//*[string() = "Exercises"]

This will return the "keyword" nodes.

Due to the Html tags which Chrome applies to XML documents, it will also return a matching number of "span.text" nodes, but just ignore those.

This example shows that you can use the string function in a predicate. When not given an argument, it will use the context node. However, string is the default data type here anyway, so you can just use the self axis instead:

//*[. = "Exercises"]

Function: number

Let's use examples here too.

Example: convert a string to a number

Run:

number("1")

You should get:

1

No surprises there. Now try:

number("some text")

You should get:

NaN

This is the number data type value which represents "Not a Number".

The number function converts strings which represent numbers into the numbers they represent, and all other strings into NaN.

Example: convert a node set to a number
Run:

number(//price)

You get the first price in the document.

The number function takes the string-value of a node set, i.e. of its first node, and converts that to a number. The example above is effectively the same as:

number(string(//price))

Exercise 76: return XML text as a number
Get the year that the book with ID "pb1" was published. Return the year as a number.

Exercise 77: filter by number values

The number function can be used in predicates and can then take the context node as its argument. Use the function to return any price nodes with a value of more than ten dollars.

Exercise 78: filter better

The number function can be used in predicates and have an argument other than the context node specified. Use the function to return the title nodes of any resources with a value of more than ten dollars.

Example: convert a Boolean to a number

Run:

    number(true())

You should get:

    1

Now run:

    Number(false())

You should get:

    0

Function: boolean

Boolean converts anything to true or false: node sets, strings, numbers. This might seem strange at first. After all, how can "chocolate" be true or false? How about the number five? How about a set of book nodes?

boolean("chocolate")

boolean(5)

boolean(//book)

In fact, all of the above are true.

Before I explain why, let's have a look at some examples of what would be false.

boolean("")

boolean(0)

boolean(//book/presenter)

That's an empty string, the number zero, and an empty node set, because books don't have presenters.

Exercise 79: spot the pattern
Can you work out what links the examples above? What makes them all false, whereas the ones before were all true?

Returning Booleans

Exercise 80: check if a node exists
Show that the first book has a price node. Return your answer as a Boolean value, i.e. true.

Exercise 81: check for child nodes
Show that the "keyword" elements do not have child elements. Return a Boolean, i.e. false.

Exercise 82: confirm an element contains text

The website has a description element. Check it contains text. Return a Boolean.

Exercise 83: confirm more simply

Do the same again, but without using data type functions.

Exercise 84: check if an element is empty

The website's format element is empty. It contains no text or child nodes. Confirm this with XPath. Return a Boolean.

Using Boolean in predicates

Unlike the other data type functions, the "boolean" function must be given an argument to convert. It doesn't default to using the context node. This doesn't stop you using the function in a predicate however.

Exercise 85: predicate syntax

Can you work out how you would use boolean in a predicate?

Try to get all the books for which a price node exists.

Exercise 86: find empty elements

List any empty elements which are descendants of website.

3.9 - Number Functions

Rounding functions

There are three functions used to round numbers. All of them return whole numbers, or "integers". There is no rounding to, for example, two decimal places.

Function: floor

You can think of "floor" as working in the same way as the floors of a building. If you're on the first floor of a building, you might be a bit higher than the carpet physically is, but, even if you stand on a stepladder, your floor number is still "one". There is no first-and-a-half floor.

Run:

    floor(1.5)

The floor function rounds down to the nearest integer.

Now run:

    floor(1.1)

    floor(1.99)

    floor(1)

You will get "1" every time.

How does floor handle negative numbers? Well, if you stand on a step ladder in the sub-basement, you could say that you are one-and-a-half floors below ground. However, you are still on floor number minus two.

Run:

floor(-1.5)

It returns "-2".

In summary, floor rounds down to the nearest integer less than, or equal to, its argument.

Function: ceiling

Ceiling, as you might guess, is the opposite of floor. Rather than go over the same ideas again, see if you can predict how ceiling works.

Exercise 87: predict how ceiling works

What would you expect the return values to be for the following?

ceiling(1.5)

ceiling(1)

ceiling(-1.5)

Function: round

Run:

round(1.1)

round(1.9)

You will get the results as "1" and "2". Round returns the nearest integer, whether above or below its argument.

Run:

round(1.5)

You will get "2". Round will round up if there is no nearest integer.

Exercise 88: prediction - 1

What would you expect the expression below to return?

    round(-1.5)

Exercise 89: prediction - 2

Look at the XPath below. What would you expect it return?

    Round(-0.5)

Run it and see. The result may surprise you.

Exercise 90: prep work

Return the first price node in the document. We'll round the price in the next exercise. For now, we just need to get the single node.

Exercise 91: rounding a node value

Get the first price in the document, round it, and return the result.

Exercise 92: shorten it

There is a simpler XPath that gives the same result. Can you work out what it is?

Exercise 93: more type conversions

What do you think the following XPaths will return? Try them out and see.

    round("5.5")

```
round("abc")
```

Exercise 94: implications
As shown above, XPath automatically converts data to the expected
type. What do you think the consequences of this are?

Rounding to two decimal places

Suppose you can get 10% off all books. Let's see what the price of
the first book will be.

Run:

```
//book/price * 0.9
```

That's a very long decimal. The number at the far end of it shouldn't
be there either.

Due to the way computers store decimal numbers, they can be
inaccurate.

Exercise 95: round to two decimal places

Get the discounted price, in dollars and cents, i.e. to two decimal
places.

Function: sum

The sum function takes a node set as an argument, and adds up all
the values in it. You could use it, for example, to calculate the cost
of buying all the resources listed in the document.

Exercise 96: use sum

Calculate the cost of buying all the resources listed in the document.

3.10 - Using XPath with Html

XPath works with Html the same way as it does with XML. However, Chrome handles XML and Html documents differently.

Chrome formats XML documents using Html. This affects how we use XPath with them. We have to work around the Html, to avoid returning it. Typically, we use "//" to navigate to an XML node, such as the XML root element, and then navigate onwards.

Chrome leaves Html documents as they are. This gives us more options. We'll explore those later in the chapter. First though, we'll do a couple of exercises to show how to use XPath on an Html page.

Exercise 97: using XPath on Html
Open "WebPage.html".

Right-click on the page and select "View page source".

This will open a new tab where you can see the structure of the Html. You will see that Html has its own set of elements: "li" for list item, "div" for division, "p" for paragraph, and so on.

This may help you plan your XPath expressions. You will still need to run the XPath in the console of your original browser tab though.

Run:

    string(//h1)

This returns the text of the "h1" element, i.e. the main header.

Exercise 98: return some elements
Use XPath to return the "div" elements.

Exercise 99: roots

To get the root element in an Html document, we can do this:

    /*

The root element is the Html element.

Can you change the XPath to return the root *node*?

Exercise 100: absolute XPaths

When you work with Html in Chrome (or XML elsewhere) you don't have to start every XPath with "//". You can navigate directly from the root node. An XPath which does this is known as an absolute XPath.

Try to return the main "div" element, the one which contains all the others, without using "//".

Absolute XPath benefits

You may now be thinking: why would anyone want to use an absolute XPath? Wouldn't it be quicker and easier to just start every XPath with "//"?

Using "//" at the start of an XPath means every node descended from the root gets searched for matching nodes. Using an absolute XPath allows a much more specific search, meaning the computer does less work. It makes your XPath faster and more efficient.

3.11 - Axes

You already covered five axes:

child

parent

attribute

descendant-or-self

self

You also covered the syntax for their use.

In navigation:

/axis::nodetest

In predicates:

[axis::nodetest]

This syntax works for all the axes. It's worth knowing, because the remaining axes don't have any associated shorthand. You have to use their full names and syntax.

The following chapters will introduce those other axes, plus a bit more on descendant-or-self.

I have split the axes into two groups: document axes and tree axes. These terms are my own and are not official or recognized in any way. We'll cover the document axes next and the tree axes later in the book.

3.12 - Document axes

There are two of these:

following

preceding

They work independently of the normal node tree structure.

Run:

//audiobook/following::*

Notice how it returns a huge list of nodes. Some of these are the Html nodes which Chrome added to the webpage in order to format and style the XML file in the browser.

The "following" axis returns, in document order, nodes which begin after the context node ends. It ignores nesting. All nodes, whether nested or not, are included. For element nodes, this means every element with its opening tag after the context node's closing tag. That's why the Html elements are included in the results.

We can get a more specific result.

Run:

//audiobook/following::*[parent::index]

This limits our results to the other resources.

Run:

//audiobook/preceding::*

The "preceding" axis is the opposite of the "following" axis. Whereas "following" starts at the end of the context node and moves down, "preceding" starts at the beginning of the context node and moves up.

The "preceding" axis returns, in *reverse* document order, nodes which end before the context node begins. It ignores nesting. All nodes, whether nested or not, are included. For element nodes, this means every element with its closing tag before the context node's opening tag. That, again, includes Html elements.

As before, we can get a more specific result.

Run:

  //audiobook/preceding::*[parent::index]

This limits our results to the other resources. As you will see, they are returned in reverse document order.

Example: use in predicates
Run:

  //index/*[following::audiobook]

This returns the child elements of index which have one or more audiobook nodes following them. It returns them in document order. It returns the same nodes as the previous XPath, but in document order.

Why to use them
These axes let you return nodes before or after another node in the document, regardless of how they are nested.

The "preceding" axis also lets you return nodes in reverse order.

Exercises

Returning a mixture of XML and Html nodes would be confusing, so we will use an Html document for these exercises.

Open "WebPage.html".

Exercise 101: get items after a node

Get all the list items, that is, "li" elements, for animals not found globally, i.e. all the ones after dolphins.

Exercise 102: get items before a node

Get all the list items before dolphins. What is the last item in the node set returned?

Exercise 103: get items before a node - 2

Get all the list items before dolphins, in document order.

Exercise 104: get items between two nodes

Get all the list items for animals after dolphins and before koala bears.

Exercise 105: reversing node order

Suppose you want to list a document's nodes in reverse order. XPath doesn't provide an explicit way to control the order of the node set you return. You can still do it though.

Write an XPath to return the list items, from bottom to top.

3.13 - String Functions

There are nine string functions. I will introduce them in three groups, according to their use. String functions may be used to:

Check for one string within another

Get part of a string

Do something else

The XML document for this chapter is Customers.xml. It only contains one customer, to keep things simple. The focus here is on how the functions work, rather than on XML navigation.

Check for one string within another

Two functions check for one string within another:

starts-with

contains

Both of these take two string arguments:

A string to look in

A string to look for

Run this example:

starts-with("word","w")

This looks in "word" for "w". It looks at the start of the string "word" only. It finds "w" and returns true.

Run this example:

contains("word","or")

This looks in "word" for "or". It looks at the whole of the string "word". It finds "or" and returns true.

You can also use XPath expressions in either argument, or both, for each function. For example, in customers.xml:

starts-with(//postcode,"SW")

This checks if the address is in South-West London, the "SW" postcode district.

Exercise 106: check text - 1a
Check if the phone number is for a mobile phone, i.e. does it start with "07"?

Exercise 107: check text - 1b
Check the email isn't obviously invalid. Does it contain the "@" symbol?

Exercise 108: check text - 1c
Check if the email contains the customer's surname.

Exercise 109: check text - 1d
Check if the surname is in the top five English surnames: Smith, Jones, Williams, Taylor and Davies.

Note: this doesn't need to be a perfect solution, just one that will be right most of the time.

Note

I realise that filtering by surname is a bit of a contrived example. A business would be more likely to filter by a customer's city, or state, or by whether their country is on the list of EU countries. However, the technique would be the same.

Check for one string within another: filtering

It's possible to use the above functions inside predicates.

For example:

```
//customer[starts-with(//postcode,"SW")]
```

This returns customers whose postcodes are in South-West London. It returns the node, rather than the Booleans we got earlier.

What if we wanted the postcodes themselves?

The self axis is useful here:

```
//postcode[starts-with(.,"SW")]
```

Exercise 110: check text - 2a

Find any mobile phone numbers, i.e. those starting with "07".

Exercise 111: check text - 2b

Check for emails which *are* obviously invalid: those which *don't* contain the "@" symbol.

You should get an empty set.

Exercise 112: check text - 2c

Get any customer whose email contains their surname.

Get any customers with surnames in the top five English surnames: Smith, Jones, Williams, Taylor and Davies.

Again, a perfect solution is not required here. We'll cover how to perfect this technique later.

The side effects of string-value

If you run:

```
//customer[contains(.,"@")]
```

You might be surprised that it returns the customer node. After all, the "@" is in the email node. However, the function expects string arguments, and we used the self axis ".", to give it the customer node. This means that XPath will take the string-value of the customer node and use that. The string-value includes the text of the customer node's descendants. The function therefore searches all the text within the customer element for "@", finds it, and returns true.

Get part of a string

Three functions get part of a string:

substring-before

substring-after

substring

The first two functions each take two string arguments:

A string to look in

A string to look for

Run this example:

substring-before("some text","e")

This looks in "some text" for "e". It finds the first "e" and returns the characters before it: "som".

Now run this example:

substring-after("some text","e")

This looks in "some text" for "e". It finds the first "e" and returns the characters after it: " text".

Note: the space character, " ", before "text", is returned just like any other character.

If you wanted to get the part of the string after the second "e", you could do this:

substring-after(substring-after("some text","e"),"e")

This gives you "xt". The inner function returns " text" as an argument to the outer function.

You can also use the function more precisely by using a longer target string:

substring-after("some text","te")

This also gives you "xt"

You can also use XPath expressions to provide the arguments. You can try that out in the next few exercises.

Exercise 114: get a partial string - 1
The part of the postcode before the space is the "outer" postcode district. Return that.

Exercise 115: get a partial string - 2

The part of the email address after the "@" sign is the domain. Return that.

Exercise 116: get a partial string - 3

The part of the date between the dashes is the month. Return that.

Exercise 117: filter by a partial string

You can use the substring functions in predicates too.

Return the customer node(s) which have email addresses in the domain "example.com".

Patterns

Below are four string functions and their arguments:

starts-with (look-in, look-for)

contains (look-in, look-for)

substring-before (look-in, look-for)

substring-after (look-in, look-for)

Notice the pattern?

The function arguments are in a consistent order. Noticing this makes it easier to remember how to use them.

Note: these argument names are not "official" in any way. The XPath specification doesn't include argument names, so I had to invent some.

Now let's look at the next function:

substring(look-in, look-for, take)

Great! It follows the same pattern. At least it will be easy to remember the order of the arguments.

The similarity ends there, however. For example, after the "look-in" argument, the substring function takes two number arguments, not strings. How does the function make any use of those?

It uses the numbers by treating the "look-in" string as a series of characters. Take the example below:

substring("abcdefg",2,5)

This returns "bcdef".

It *looks for* character number two within the series, and *takes* five characters from that position onwards.

Take this example:

substring("abcdefg",3,2)

This returns "cd".

It looks for character number three within the series, and takes two characters from that position onwards.

Exercise 118: get a partial string - 4
Return the month from date-of-birth. Use the substring function.

Exercise 119: get a partial string - 5
Now return the same month as a number.

Do something else

There are four miscellaneous string functions:

translate

normalize-space

concat

string-length

I'll introduce each one with a simple example to show what it does and then take a more in-depth look at its uses and behaviour.

Function: translate

Exercise 120: prediction - 1

The arguments of this function are:

translate(look-in, look-for, replace-with)

Knowing the above, can you guess what will happen when you run

translate("old dog", "old", "new")

Exercise 121: prediction - 2

Guess what will happen when you run:

translate("old dog", "old", "")

Now run it and see what happens.

Exercise 122: remove a character

Return the telephone number, without any spaces in.

Note the capital letter in the XPath below. What will happen if you run it?

    translate("Old dog", "old", "new")

Make an XPath that checks if the city is "LONDON", whatever case the characters are in.

Function: normalize-space

Run:

    normalize-space("old dog")

The function returns exactly what you put in.

Now run it again, but put a few extra spaces before, after and between the words. You get the same string you got back last time. The extra spaces are gone.

This function "normalizes" whitespace in strings. This means that, for any string you give it, the function:

removes any whitespace characters from the start

removes any whitespace characters from the end

converts any remaining sequences of whitespace characters into single spaces.

If you pull text from nodes, this function can tidy it up.

What would you expect to get back when you run the XPath below? Once you have decided, run it and find out.

    normalize-space(//name)

Get the address of the customer as a single-line string.

Get the entire text content of the customer as a single-line string.

Function: concat

Run:

    concat("ab","cd","ef")

You get "abcdef". This function joins two or more strings into one.

Exercise 128: join strings

Get the full name of the customer, as one string.

Note: joining an unknown number of strings

One of the limitations of this function is that you have to specify each string, or each node, individually. You can't for example, give it a node set, like the keywords of all the books in "resources.xml", and have it return them as a single string. The function only works on arguments provided individually, as in the example above.

In fact, the XPath 1.0 specification doesn't provide a function to join the strings of a node set in this way.

Combining functions

Earlier, we had an exercise:

Check if the surname is in the top five English surnames.

The XPath to answer it was:

contains("Smith Jones Williams Taylor Davies",//surname)

The problem with that was:

It allowed false positives, like "Tay", i.e. partial word matches.

One way to avoid this problem would be to use:

//surname="Smith" or //surname="Williams" or... (etc, etc)

The problem with that is:

It's really long.

There is a way to use the "concat" function to make the shorter XPath reliable. See if you can figure it out.

Exercise 129: match a string against a list.

Make the XPath below work reliably.

contains("Smith Jones Williams Taylor Davies",//surname)

There are two steps to doing this.

Hint: the first step: start by adding spaces to the beginning and end of the first argument, i.e.

contains(" Smith Jones Williams Taylor Davies ",//surname)

The beginning and end of each possible match are now marked by space characters.

Exercise 130: adapt
Suppose you were checking against a list of cities, and some of them had spaces in the names. For example, if your XPath was:

contains(" New York Boston Philadelphia ",concat(" ",//city," "))

How would you change the above to stop it matching the English city of York?

As a first step, replace "//city" with "York":

contains(" New York Boston Philadelphia ",concat(" ","York"," "))

Then you can test any other changes you make.

Function: string-length
Run:

string-length("abcd")

You get the number four. This function counts the number of characters in a string.

Exercise 131: get string length
Get the number of characters in the postcode.

Exercise 132: investigate the function
From the last example, you might think this function is very simple. Mostly, it is. However, run the XPath below:

string-length(//contact)

You will get quite a large character count returned. It is higher, in fact, than the sum of the number of characters in the two child elements. Can you work out why?

Exercise 133: filter by string length
You can use this function in a predicate. Its argument is optional. If no argument is given, the context node is used instead.

Find any elements inside the customer element which contain less than two characters.

Exercise 134: check a postcode is within its character limit
No UK postcode should be more than seven characters, excluding spaces. Write an XPath that confirms the postcode is not too long.

3.14 - Tree axes

These fall into three pairs.

Sibling axes:

    following-sibling

    preceding-sibling

Descendant axes:

    descendant

    descendant-or-self

Ancestor axes:

    ancestor

    ancestor-or-self

The following chapters will cover each of the pairs above.

3.15 - Sibling axes

Siblings are the child nodes of a shared parent node. They are all nested directly within the same element (assuming the parent is an element and not the root node).

Examples

Open the file "WebPage.html".

Run:

> //li[.="dogs"]/following-sibling::*

You will see the two list items after the one for "dogs", in document order, i.e. from top to bottom.

Now run:

> //li[.="hamsters"]/preceding-sibling::*

You will see the two list items before the one for "hamsters", in reverse document order, i.e. from bottom to top.

Exercise 135: use following-sibling

Can you get the animal after "red kangaroos"? Return the answer as a string.

Exercise 136: use preceding-sibling

Can you return the name of animal before "koala bears"?

Exercise 137: get a specific sibling

Can you return the name of the first animal in the list containing "koala bears"?

3.16 - Descendant axes

The descendant axis returns an element's children, and their children, and *their* children, and so on, as a node set.

The descendant-or-self axis does the same, but returns the context node too, at the start of the set. Both axes work down the page from top to bottom, i.e. in document order.

Open the file "WebPage.html".

Run:

   //*[@id="article"]/descendant::*[position() < 4]

This gets the element with the id "article" and returns its first three descendants.

Right-click on the web page and select "View page source" to see the page's Html in a new tab. In the page source, find the elements which the XPath returned.

Notice how the XPath returned the closest three descendants in the document, rather than the closest three descendants on the node tree.

That is, it didn't return the "global" div element, even though that is a child element of the "article" div. Instead, it returned a paragraph element, "p", which is a child node's child, i.e. a more distant descendant. It did this because the paragraph element came first in the document.

Exercise 138: use descendant
Write an XPath to find the article "div" and then navigate to its first paragraph, "p", and return that.

Get the div element with the id "article", and all it descendant divs.

Find a way to use "//" to get the div and its descendants.

Hint: remember what "//" is shorthand for. Remember that child is only the default axis.

3.17 - Ancestor axes

The ancestor axis returns a node's parent, and its parent, and *its* parent, and so on, as a node set.

The ancestor-or-self axis does the same, but returns the context node too, at the start of the set. Both axes work up the page, i.e. in reverse document order.

Examples
Run:

> //li[. = "hamsters"]/ancestor::node()

This finds the hamsters list item and returns a node set starting with its parent and ending with the root element, "html", and then the root node, "document".

Now run:

> //li[. = "hamsters"]/ancestor-or-self::node()

This does the same thing, but includes the hamsters list item element at the start of the set returned.

Exercise 141: find ancestors
Write an XPath that finds the list items for any "red" animals and then navigates on to get the section headers of those items.

In this case, the section headers are the "h2" elements.

Exercise 142: filter by ancestor
Retrieve, for Asia only, any list items which contain the string "red" in their text.

3.18 - The namespace axis

As far as I can tell, this isn't actually implemented in Chrome's XPath, so we can't use it.

However, XPath provides several functions which do allow us to work with namespaces. These are implemented in Chrome. I'll introduce XML namespaces, and the functions for working with them, in later chapters.

3.19 - Node Set functions

These function fall into three groups:

    Context functions

    Namespace functions

    Other functions

Note: these groups are not "official"; the terms used here are my own.

Context functions

The context functions are:

    position

    last

We covered these at the start of the book.

Namespace functions

The namespace functions are:

    name

    local-name

    namespace-uri

We will cover these in their own chapter, after the chapters which explain how XML namespaces work.

Other functions

The other functions are:

    count

id

We will cover these here.

The "count()" function takes a node set as an argument and counts it. Suppose we have some example XML:

```
<this>

    <that>???</that>

    <that>???</that>

</this>
```

I never said it was sensible XML. Anyway, we can run:

```
count(//that)
```

That returns two.

Now let's run:

```
count(//this)
```

This returns one.

Exercise 143: count the nodes

In the resources file, count the total number of keyword elements for the books.

Note: the id function

The id function is used to select elements from an XML document.

However, it only works on XML documents with a unique ID attribute type declared in the document type definition.

Also, as far as I can tell, the function isn't actually implemented in XPath in Chrome, so we can't use it anyway.

Note

The following sections are about XML namespaces. If you are learning XPath for use with Html and browser test automation, they won't be relevant to you. You may wish to skip them and go to section six. See the table of contents for a link on your e-reader or, for paperback readers, the page number.

4 - XML Namespaces

4.1 - Names and namespaces

Namespaces are often added to XML. An XPath which works on plain XML can fail on that same XML once a namespace is added. For this reason, it is useful to understand how XML namespaces work and how to deal with them in XPath. The next three chapters are intended to help you do that.

This chapter covers some basics of XML namespaces: like what they are and why they are used. It covers the difference between default namespaces and namespace prefixes. It shows how to identify each and how they affect XPath.

The following chapter is a brief jargon-buster. It defines, and explains the differences between, local names, namespace names, namespace prefixes, qualified names, expanded names, and non-colonized names.

The final chapter introduces the various XPath functions for working with names and namespaces. It shows how to navigate namespaced XML and how to retrieve namespaces used within XML.

XML Namespaces

XML namespaces identify node types uniquely by providing extra context. The uniqueness is provided by something called a URI, which I will cover later. For now, let's focus on that extra context.

What does context mean? If someone says "basket" do you know what type of basket they mean? Do they want to carry their shopping in it or throw a ball through it? How about "rocket"? Is it something they saw at a fireworks display, or the latest news on SpaceX? Without a context, the words are vague. With context, they are clear.

Just like "SpaceX" provides context for "rocket", namespaces provide context for nodes.

Default Namespaces

XML namespaces are easy to find and identify. They are found in the opening tag of elements, alongside any attributes. They are not attributes, however. Namespaces are a separate node type, all of their own. They can be distinguished from attributes because they always consist of, or begin with, "xmlns", meaning, "XML NameSpace".

    <rocket xmlns="spacex">Lift Off!</rocket>

In the above, the namespace is "spacex".

    <rocket xmlns="fireworks">Bang!</rocket>

In this case, it is "fireworks".

Exercise 144: prediction - 1

Suppose you were to search an XML document, containing the above elements, for rocket nodes:

    //rocket

Which of the two would the XPath find?

Exercise 145: prediction - 2

Suppose the rocket node has descendants.

    <rocket xmlns="fireworks">

      <colour>green</colour>

    </rocket>

Would the XPath below return any nodes?

    //colour

Exercise 146: identify a node's namespace using defaults

Suppose "colour" has a closer ancestor node, and the default namespace is set for that.

    <rocket xmlns="fireworks">

      <effects xmlns="pyrotechnics">

        <colour>green</colour>

        <type>sparkly</type>

      </effects>

    </rocket>

Which namespace(s) is the colour node in?

Namespace Prefixes

Often, namespaced nodes will look like this:

    <f:rocket xmlns:f="fireworks">Bang!</f:rocket>

If they have "xmlns" followed by a colon, ":", the text after the colon, in this case, "f", becomes the namespace prefix. It may seem strange that the prefix appears at the end of "xmlns", but the "f" isn't a prefix to the namespace node. It's a prefix put in front of other node names to link them to the namespace. Within rocket and its descendant nodes, if any, the prefix "f" can be used to represent the namespace "fireworks".

In the example above, the node name "rocket" has been prefixed with "f", plus a colon to separate them. As the XML above also

117

declares "f" the namespace prefix for "fireworks", this puts the rocket node in the fireworks namespace.

Unlike the "xmlns=" examples shown earlier, namespaces declared using prefixes do not replace the default namespace. They only apply when the prefix is actually used, as in the next exercise.

Exercise 147: identify node namespaces by prefix

Suppose we have a company supplying materials to both the space industry and the fireworks industry, and they use XML, with namespaces.

```
<s:rocket xmlns:s="space">

    <material>titanium</material>

    <material>carbon-fibre</material>

    <s:material>space paint</s:material>

</s:rocket>

<f:rocket xmlns:f="fireworks">

    <f:material>rocket-casing</f:material>

    <material>fuses</material>

    <material>gunpowder</material>

</f:rocket>
```

Can you tell which namespaces apply to which nodes?

Attribute Namespaces

Attributes nodes have namespaces too. They can be given a namespace by prefix, as below.

```
<f:material @f:sizing="large" @regulated="no">rocket-
casing</f:material>
```

In this example, the "sizing" attribute is prefixed, so it is namespaced. The "regulated" attribute isn't prefixed, so it isn't namespaced.

Namespace URIs

The namespaces used in the above examples are not typical. Normally, namespaces are defined uniquely, using a URI.

The URI, or Uniform Resource Identifier, is typically, though not always, a URL, Uniform Resource Locator, i.e. a web address, for example:

github.com/author-d-armstrong/xpath/fireworks

github.com/author-d-armstrong/xpath/spacex

In a real-life XML document, it would look like this:

```
<f:rocket xmlns:f="github.com/author-d-
armstrong/xpath/fireworks">Bang!</f:rocket>
```

4.2 - XML Names – Terminology

Local name

This is the type of name you already use! Every element or attribute node has a local name. This is the same as the "local part" of its name. It is often the complete name of the node.

Example: rocket

Namespace, Namespace Name, Namespace-URI

All three of these terms mean the same thing. The namespace is a unique string, which provides a way to group nodes, which may have the same local names, into unique categories.

Example: github.com/author-d-armstrong/xpath/fireworks

Prefix name, Namespace prefix

This is the string which is defined after the colon following "xmlns", if there is one.

The same string is used before the colon in the element or attribute name itself.

The format is: prefix:local name

Example: f

(as used in "f:rocket")

The prefix represents the namespace and provides a convenient, shorthand way to include it within the text of node names.

QName, Qualified Name

The QName is the prefix followed by a colon followed by the local name. It represents the expanded name, which we'll cover next.

The QName is what you would see on a prefixed node. The node could be an element or an attribute.

Example: f:rocket

Expanded name:
This is the namespace name, followed by the local name.

You won't see this in an XML document. This is something that the software processing the XPath will infer, e.g. from the namespace prefix and the local name.

The expanded name uniquely identifies the node type.

NCName, Non-colonized name
Non-colonized isn't a reference to Mars before SpaceX gets there. It's actually non-*colon*-ized, i.e. a name without colons. Rather than a specific type of name with a defined purpose in XML, this simply refers to a name format.

Both the namespace prefix and the local part of a name must be NC names. They must not contain colons because a colon is the character used to separate the prefix from the local part of the name.

5 - XPath for working with namespaces

5.1 - XPath Name Functions

These are the functions in XPath that return name-related data. This section explains how those functions relate to the various types of XML names.

Open the "rockets.xml" file to begin.

Function: local-name()

This give the local part of a node's name.

For example, from the node "<f:rocket />" it would return the string "rocket".

Function: namespace-uri()

This gives the namespace of a node's expanded name.

For example, in our document, from the node "<f:rocket />" it would return the string "github.com/author-d-armstrong/xpath/fireworks".

Function: name()

This gives the QNAME of a node.

This includes the prefix and the local part.

For example, from the node "<f:rocket />" it would return the string "f:rocket".

How to use these functions

Each of the functions above works in the same way. The only difference is the part of the name they return. The examples below show how they work.

Retrieving name data from nodes

To get the first child element of the products node, you would run:

    //products/*[1]

We can use this node as an argument in the functions above.

Run:

local-name(//products/*[1])

namespace-uri(//products/*[1])

name(//products/*[1])

See what you get!

Exercise 148: get a product by attribute value
Get the element for the product with the ID of 34.

This exercise is just here to set up the next one. You don't need to use any functions for this part.

Exercise 149: find an element's namespace
Get the namespace URI for the product with the ID of 34.

Exercise 150: find an attribute
Get the product ID attribute with the value of 34.

This exercise is also just set-up for the next one. You don't need to use any functions for this part.

Exercise 151: find an attribute's namespace
Get the namespace URI for the ID attribute with the value of 34.

Exercise 152: find an attribute – part 2
Try to get the product size attribute with the value of "small" the same way as you did for product ID. Does it work? Why / why not?

Run:

> //products/rocket

This returns no matches.

Generic node tests, like "*", still work as normal.

Run:

> //products/*

This matches all the child elements in products, regardless of namespace.

To deal with namespaced nodes, we can use generic node tests to match them, and the three name functions to filter those matches.

The next two sections show how to do that. You can use functions to find nodes *despite* their namespaces. You can use functions to find nodes *by* their namespaces.

Retrieving nodes despite namespaces

The three name functions can all be used inside predicates.

Like many functions, if you don't specify an argument, they use the context node, as in the example below.

Run:

> //products/*[name() = "f:rocket"]

This gets you all the rocket elements in the fireworks namespace.

Often though, namespaces are not relevant to what you are doing, and you just need a way to make your XPath ignore them.

Exercise 153: get elements despite namespaces

Can you work out how to get all the rocket elements from the document, whatever their namespace?

Hint: use "local-name()".

Exercise 154: get attributes despite namespaces

Get all the product size attribute nodes from the document, whatever their namespace.

Exercise 155: find an element by attribute value, despite namespaces

Find the product with a size of small.

Exercise 156: find out the namespace of an element

Find out the namespace of the small product.

Other ways to bypass namespaces

In SQL Server you can use "*" as a wildcard, to match any namespace, like this:

```
//*:rocket
```

This would match rocket nodes in any namespace.

Retrieving nodes by namespaces

So far, we have covered how to find the local name and namespace of a node. We have covered how to find a node despite its namespace, by using local-name. Now, we will cover how to find nodes by their namespaces using namespace-uri.

For example, to get only the space rocket node(s), you could use:

//*[local-name() = "rocket" and namespace-uri() = "github.com/author-d-armstrong/xpath/space"]

Exercise 157: find elements in a specific namespace, only
Find the materials used only in fireworks.

Exercise 158: find elements not in a specific namespace
Find only the materials *not* used in fireworks.

Exercise 159: find only namespaced elements
Find the materials used only in specific industries, i.e. fireworks or space. That is, include those with namespaces specified, exclude those without.

Exercise 160: find only non-namespaced elements
Find the materials which are in the default namespace.

Keeping XPath short

Using namespaces in XPath expressions can make them very long. However, often, you can avoid that. If you know which prefixes are used for which namespaces, you can do this:

//products/*[name() = "f:rocket"]

Try it out!

Exercise 161: find specific elements in a specific namespace
Find the materials which are in the space namespace. Don't use
namespace-uri().

Exercise 162: find all elements in a specific namespace
Find the elements which are in the space namespace. Don't use
namespace-uri().

Dealing with default namespaces
Sometimes a namespace node looks like this:

  xmlns="something"

This resets the default namespace in the element where it is found,
and in any descendants, unless they also reset the default namespace.

You can still navigate these namespaces. You just have to work out
which namespaces apply to which nodes.

Open the rocketsDefaultNamespace.xml file to begin.

Exercise 163: find elements in a specific default namespace
Find the elements which are in the space namespace.

Exercise 164: find only non-namespaced elements
Find the materials, if any, which are in the document's default
namespace.

Exercise 165: check how default namespace affect attributes

Write an XPath to show whether the product ID attributes share their element node's default namespace.

---

6 - Automatic XPath Generators

6.1 - Is there a tool to auto-generate XPath?

Chrome has just such a tool built in. You can use it as follows:

Exercise 166: using "Copy XPath" in Chrome

Open "webpage.html" in Chrome.

We'll generate an XPath for the first list item, the one that says "dogs".

Right-click on that item.

On the context menu, click "Inspect".

A panel will appear, containing the Html source code for the page. In that panel, the code for the list item will be highlighted.

Right click on the highlighted area.

A context menu will appear.

On the context menu, click "Copy".

On the submenu, click "Copy XPath".

Paste the XPath somewhere, e.g. a text editor like Notepad, so you can read it.

Uses of "Copy XPath"

This tool auto-generates an XPath to a specific element, directly from a web page. You can use the XPath to navigate to the element.

If you are automating a browser test, e.g. with Selenium, this is very helpful. Selecting an element on a webpage is one of the most common things to automate. You might select a form field to fill in, a button to click, or a link to follow.

There are several ways to select an element: notably by name, ID, or XPath. However, not all elements have names or IDs. In those cases, you can use XPath, and "Copy XPath" is the easiest way to do it.

Another use of "Copy XPath" is to get an XPath that approximates what you want, and then modify it.

Limits of "Copy XPath"

Html only

The XPath copied does not work for XML files opened in Chrome. Chrome formats these files using Html, and the XPath copied applies only to that Html. The XML within them is treated as text content.

Of course, that doesn't mean there are no other tools out there to auto-generate XPath from XML files. It just means you can't do it using Chrome itself.

Singular

The XPath copied is to a single element. If you want a way to select multiple elements, you can't do it just by using "Copy XPath".

Navigational

The XPath copied is intended for specifying elements. You can't copy an XPath that, for example, returns the value of an element, rounded to the nearest whole number.

Automated

How can automation be a weakness?

The XPath you generated earlier selected the list item by its position. However, you may have wanted the list item which contained "dogs". If the web page was edited to move dogs down, you would still want "dogs", but the XPath would give you the "cats" item.

If you wrote an XPath manually, you could have it select the element by its text content. The XPath would then work, even if the list was reordered.

The tool doesn't know why you are choosing an element. It automatically chooses a way to get it, but how it does so may not reflect what you want.

Static

The XPath you get by copying from Chrome treats the web page as static. However, web pages are often dynamic. The copied XPath is correct for its element at the time, but, later, it may not be.

Here's one example. Imagine a shopping website's delivery page. When a delivery option, e.g. "next day" is selected, the page changes to highlight that option.

A copied XPath could navigate to the element. Once the page changes, the XPath may go somewhere else, or return an empty node set.

That is, the same XPath may work once and then fail on re-use.

Now, imagine you use a copied XPath to make an automated browser test. You want to simulate a customer choosing a delivery option.

What happens if the website saves the last delivery option selected? If the page is re-opened, it opens with "next day" pre-selected. The test may be run once and pass. Then it may be re-run, perhaps on a different occasion, and fail, because the web page was different each time, and the XPath was copied from only one version of the same web page.

If you write an XPath manually instead, you can choose how it navigates and so make it more reliable.

The XPath provided navigates the page as a whole, i.e. from the root. If you want a way to navigate from one element to another, "Copy XPath" won't be enough.

Why would you need to navigate between elements?

Imagine that delivery web page again. You want your test program to automatically select a delivery option according to the text, e.g. "next day delivery", in the option's label element.

Your test will run several times. Each time, it will select a different delivery option. However, the text is in a label element, i.e. separate from the button the user actually clicks on, so you need the test software to click on the button *next to* that element.

You need some manual XPath skills here for two reasons.

First, you need an XPath to find an element (the label) by checking if its text contains a value, not by relying on its position.

Second, you then need to find an element by its position *relative* to the label. You can do this by extending the XPath to navigate onwards, from the label, to the button element.

This also results in a better test. Navigating to each element of a web page in isolation doesn't simulate user behaviour. Clicking a button next to a description does.

Conclusion

Tools for auto-generating XPath are fast but are of limited use. It can be risky to rely on them. Ideally, their use needs to be backed up by an understanding of the XPath they produce and the skill to modify it. Hopefully, this book has provided both of those.

Afterword

Author's note

I do hope you found this book useful. I write books in an exercise-based format because I believe it's a better way to learn.

If you found the book useful, please leave me a good review. That way other people will know to buy it too.

If you feel the book could be improved in some way, please let me know at:

authordarmstrong@gmail.com

Answers

No answer 1 - not a problem-solving exercise

No answer 2 - not a problem-solving exercise

No answer 3 - not a problem-solving exercise

No answer 4 - not a problem-solving exercise

No answer 5 - not a problem-solving exercise

Answer 6

$x('//book')

If you ran the XPath above, it returned a set of nodes listed inside square brackets. The Chrome console also displays the ID of each node in the set.

In the console, expand that set.

The nodes will now be displayed on separate lines.

If you want to, you can now expand and explore any of them, as you did with the index node.

Answer 7

[ ]

This result is an empty set. It shows that there are no magazine nodes in the document.

However, the XPath was intended to return a node set, so it does, even when the set is empty. Whether an XPath returns zero, one, or many nodes, it returns them as a set.

No answer 8 - not a problem-solving exercise

Answer 9

```
$x('//book[position() = 1]')
```

Explanation: predicates

The "position() = 1" above is an example of a predicate. A predicate is a condition against which nodes are checked, before they are returned. They allow you to "filter" your results. In XPath, predicates are written inside square brackets.

A predicate is applied to each node in turn. In this case, the "position()" function is run for each node in the set. The function returns the node's position within the set, as a number. This number is known as the context position. If the context position for a node makes the predicate condition true, i.e. "1 = 1", then the node is returned.

For now, we'll use only position-based predicates. This allows us to filter node sets down to single nodes, which provides simpler examples to learn from. Also, the shorthand version, which we're about to cover, makes them easy to use.

Shorthand

The expression above can be shortened to:

```
$x('//book[1]')
```

This works because, by default, when a predicate is given a number value, it compares it against the output of the "position()" function.

Note

This example makes "//" and context position seem very simple. They way they work is actually a bit more complex than first appears. We'll cover "//" in more detail later in the section. We'll cover context and context position in the *Predicates* chapter.

Answer 10

    //video/metadata/keyword

We can use the same approach to get book keywords:

    //book/metadata/keyword

However, as there are multiple books, each is used as a context node, one after another, and we get all the keywords. We need to filter.

    //book[1]/metadata/keyword

This gets just the keywords from the first book.

Answer 11

    //book[1]/metadata/keyword[2]

The node's text should be "XML".

Answer 12

    //book[2]/metadata/keyword[1]

The node's text should be "Cmd Line".

Answer 13
//video/node()

Notice that this returns non-element nodes, like text nodes, too.

Answer 14
//index/*

We know that all the resource nodes are elements, so we can use "*" here.

Answer 15
//narrator/parent::*

Answer 16
//book[last()]/title

Answer 17
//book[last()]/@lang

Answer 18
//book/@lang

This XPath finds all the books nodes, then follows the attribute axis for each of them, matching any attributes of type "lang".

Answer 19
As all the resources are children of the "index" node, we can use:

//index/*/@lang

In this case, as language attributes are only on the resource nodes (book, video, etc), we can use:

//@lang

This gets any "lang" attributes in the document.

Answer 20
//@*

Answer 21
//video/@*[last()]

Answer 22
//series/parent::*

Shorthand
That's a lot of typing though. Try using:

//series/..

The ".." is shorthand for:

parent::node()

It's important to know the full axis syntax too though. Some axes don't have any shorthand associated with them.

Answer 23
//narrator/..

Answer 24

//processing-instruction()

Answer 25

//video/node()

Notice that the comments and text nodes *are* included.

Answer 26

//video/*

Notice that the comments and text nodes are *not* included.

Answer 27

//video/comment()

Answer 28

//video/title/text()

Answer 29

//video/text()

Notice anything about the text in these text nodes? It's all whitespace. This Xpath selects child nodes of video, so it only selects text nodes *between* element nodes (and comment nodes). The video's title, for example, is not selected because it's *within* another element node. It isn't a child of "video"; it's a child of "title".

Answer 30
No. This returns multiple nodes.

Answer 31
//book[1]/metadata/keyword[1]

Answer 32
//book[1]//keyword[1]

We can also use "//" in the middle of an XPath. It returns all descendants of the context node. It lets us shorten and simplify XPath expressions.

Answer 33
//index/*[url]

Answer 34
//index/*[comment()]

Answer 35
//index/*[@id]

Answer 36
//*[@lang]

Answer 37

[ ]

It returns an empty set. If there is no price node, then there is no price node with a value less than 10.

Answer 38

//book[price > 10]

Answer 39

//*[metadata/keyword = "Selenium"]

Answer 40

//*[@lang = "English"]

Answer 41

//*[@lang = "English"]/title

Answer 42

//book[price < 10]/price

You can do this, but it's a bit inefficient to go back and forth between book and price nodes like this. There is a better way. A predicate can refer to the value of the node it filters.

Example:

//book/price[. < 10]

This gets any price node with a value below $10.

How does this work? It works because "." is shorthand for:

self::node()

The self axis returns the context node, in this case, the price node.

By default, a predicate would use the child axis. With the self axis, however, you can apply the predicate to the same nodes you are using it to filter.

Answer 43

Nothing – the self axis returns the same node it starts from.

Answer 44

//price[. < 5]

Answer 45

//index/*[metadata/keyword]

Answer 46

//index/*[metadata/keyword[last()] = "Testing"]

Answer 47

//index/*[metadata/keyword[3]]

This predicate (the outer one) checks for the presence of a third keyword in each resource's metadata.

Answer 48
  //book[not(position() = last())]

Answer 49
  //index/*[not(url)]

Answer 50
  //index/*[not(price)]

Answer 51
  //index/*[not(price > 10)]

Note

This is not the same as getting all resources with prices below $10. The XPath above also returns resources which don't have a price node at all.

Answer 52
  //title[lang("en-us")]

Answer 53
  //*[lang("en")]

This XPath also returns elements without an "xml:lang" attribute. That's because those elements have inherited their language from the "file" element, their ancestor. Descendants share their ancestor's language, unless it is overwritten using "xml:lang", as it is in the other titles.

//title[not(lang("en"))]

This returns the nodes for book titles which are not in English. The "lang" function returns a Boolean into the "not" function, and the "not" function returns the opposite Boolean.

//book[position() < 3]

OR

//book[position() <= 2]

//book[position() != last()]

//book[price = 0]

This works as long as the free books have a price specified. However, some resources, such as the website, are free and don't have a price node at all.

//index/*[not(price!=0)]

This XPath checks for resources which don't have a non-zero price node.

Answer 59

   //book[1]/price – 2.50

Note: when using the subtraction operator, "-", after a node name, using spaces matters.

For example, run:

   //book[1]/price–2.50

This returns an empty set. Without the spaces around the operator, XPath interprets "price-2.50" as the name of the node to look for.

Answer 60

   //book[last() - 1]

Answer 61

   //book[price div 2 < 10]

Answer 62

   //book[position() mod 2 = 0]

Answer 63

   //author | //presenter | //narrator

Answer 64

   //comment() | //processing-instruction()

Answer 65

(//book/metadata/keyword)[last()]

Answer 66

(//index//*)[last()]

Answer 67

(//video | //audiobook | //website)//keyword

Answer 68

//book[format = "Paperback" and price > 10]

Answer 69

//book[format = "Ebook" or format = "ebook"]

Answer 70

//book[price > 10][1]

Answer 71

//book[1][price > 10]

You probably noticed this is just the last XPath with the predicates switched around.

The order in which you chain the predicates can be important.

//book[price < 10][author = "D Armstrong"]

OR

//book[author = "D Armstrong"][price < 10]

The order in which you chain the predicates can also be unimportant.

Answer 73

string(//comment())

Answer 74

You see all the text content of the first book's descendant nodes, in the same order as on the document, including the line breaks. The function returns all content from a node and its descendants. This is known as the node's "string-value".

Answer 75

string(//index)

Answer 76

number(//book[@id="pb1"]/year)

Answer 77

//price[number() > 10]

However, you could just use the self axis:

//price[. > 10]

XPath would take the number value of the context node anyway.

//index/*[number(price) > 10]

Of course, you could also just do this:

//index/*[price > 10]

All the arguments in the second set represent the absence of a value. This isn't an official definition, but it's an easy way to remember how the function works.

By the same logic, this returns false:

boolean(NaN)

On the other hand, this returns true:

boolean(-5)

A negative value is still a value.

Also, this returns true:

boolean(" ")

Whitespace characters are not an empty string.

---

boolean(//book[1][price])

OR

boolean(//book[1]/price)

Note: this would also return false if there was no book, as the node set would still be empty.

---

boolean(//website/metadata/keyword/*)

---

boolean(string(//website/description))

If description had descendants, this would also check for text in those.

//website/description != ""

---

boolean(//website/format/node())

The node test used here covers all types of child nodes, including text nodes, which would be present if format contained any text. As it is, format is an empty element and returns an empty node set, which gets converted to "false".

//book[boolean(price)]

However, you don't need to. You can just do this:

//book[price]

//website//*[not(node())]

Again, you could use the boolean function here, but there is no need to.

The results are: 2, 1, and -1.

In summary, ceiling rounds up to the nearest integer greater than, or equal to, its argument.

-1

-0

Yes, XPath supports negative zero. It appears in some situations, e.g. this one. Mathematically speaking, it's the same value as positive zero, so I'll just point out that it exists and isn't an error and leave it at that.

(//price)[1]

Answer 91

round((//price)[1])

Answer 92

round(//price)

The function expects a number argument. If you give it a node set, it takes the first node, gets its string-value, and converts that to a number.

Answer 93

The string "5.5" becomes the number "5.5", and rounds to six.

The string "abc" becomes NaN (Not a Number) and remains that when rounded.

Answer 94

One consequence is that it prevents most type-mismatch errors. That is, if a function gets the "wrong", or an unexpected, data type from a node or a sub-expression, the XPath doesn't "crash". All data types can be converted from, and only node sets cannot be converted to. Because of this, XPath expressions can handle different inputs in a relatively robust way.

Answer 95

round((//book/price * 0.9) * 100) div 100

If you multiply by 100 before rounding, then divide again afterwards, the rounding doesn't affect the first two decimal places.

Answer 96
   sum(//price)

No answer 97 - not a problem-solving exercise

Answer 98
   //div

You may have noticed that some of the div elements are children of the other one. They are all descendants of the root node, though, so they are all returned.

Answer 99

The root node, or document node, is the root element's parent, so you can do this:

   /*/..

However, it's also the default context node when starting an XPath, so you can just do this:

   /

Try it and see.

Answer 100
   /html/body/div

Answer 101

//li[. = "dolphins"]/following::li

We find the list item with the text "dolphins", and then find list items following it.

Answer 102

//li[. = "dolphins"]/preceding::li

The last item returned is the first one on the page. The nodes are returned in reverse document order.

Answer 103

//li[following::li[. = "dolphins"]]

We check for list items followed by the dolphin list item.

Answer 104

//li[. = "dolphins"]/following::li[following::li[. = "koala bears"]]

Answer 105

(//li)[last()] | (//li)[last()]/preceding::li

We get all the list items in the document, use brackets to flatten them into a single set, and then take the last one. We use the union operator to join that node with the set of all list items preceding it.

Answer 106

starts-with(//phone,"07")

Answer 107

contains(//email,"@")

Answer 108

contains(//email,//surname)

Answer 109

contains("Smith Jones Williams Taylor Davies",//surname)

This is a little imprecise. If, for example, the surname was "Tay", the XPath would still return true. We can fix that though. We can modify the XPath so that it works reliably. I'll show how later in the chapter.

If you use the function this way, but inside a predicate, it filters out a lot of nodes which don't fit your criteria. We'll do that later.

Answer 110

//phone[starts-with(.,"07")]

Answer 111

//email[not(contains(.,"@"))]

Answer 112

//customer[contains(//email,//surname)]

//customer[contains("Smith Jones Williams Taylor Davies",//surname)]

If this document did contain multiple customers, or we needed to run the XPath against multiple XML documents, we could use this to find all the customers with a listed surname.

Answer 114

substring-before(//postcode," ")

Answer 115

substring-after(//email,"@")

Answer 116

substring-before(substring-after(//date_of_birth,"-"),"-")

Answer 117

//customer[substring-after(//email,"@") = "example.com"]

Answer 118

substring(//date_of_birth,6,2)

Answer 119

number(substring(//date_of_birth,6,2))

Answer 120

You might have expected to get the string "new dog", but instead you get, "new wng".

Why does this happen? The function doesn't find and replace whole strings; it finds and replaces characters in those strings. For "old" and "new", it replaces:

"o" with "n"

"l" with "e"

"d" with "w"

All the characters in "old dog", except the space, " ", and "g", are in the "look-for" string. They all get replaced, or "translated", with their matching characters in the "replace-with" argument.

Answer 121

You get the string " g". If the second argument is longer than the third, the extra characters are still removed, but not replaced.

Answer 122

```
translate(//phone," ","")
```

Answer 123

You get "Oew wng". The capital "O" is not replaced, as it is a different character to the lower case "o".

This is useful though. As capitals are different characters, we can also change their case in a string:

```
translate("Old dog","gold","GOLD")
```

This returns:

"OLD DOG"

We replaced all the lower case letters with their upper case equivalents.

How is this useful? XPath is case-sensitive and we often need to compare strings. For example, to check if an address is in London, we could use the XPath below:

//city = "London"

However, if the city is recorded as "LONDON", it will return false.

To do a case-insensitive comparison, we can translate the city string to uppercase first, and compare it to "LONDON".

Answer 124

translate(//city,"lond","LOND") = "LONDON"

If we were translating a longer string, we might have to use the whole alphabet in arguments two and three. It's a good thing London only has four different letters.

Answer 125

You get the full name back. The function returns the text from all the child nodes, joined together into one string, and with its whitespace normalized too.

Answer 126

normalize-space(//address)

Simple and convenient!

Answer 127

normalize-space(//customer)

As the string-value of each node includes all of its descendants, not just its children, this is all we need to do.

We could also run:

normalize-space(/)

That would input the context node XPath starts from, i.e. the root node, into the function. In fact, as the function will use the context node if an argument is not specified, we could just do this:

normalize-space()

This gives us the entire document's text on one line. It would, however, include all the text that Chrome adds into the Html.

Answer 128

concat(//first_name, " ", //surname)

The space in the second argument separates the names in the string returned.

Answer 129

contains(" Smith Jones Williams Taylor Davies ",concat(" ",//surname," "))

Use "concat" to add spaces around the second argument.

Now, all matches must start and end with a space, meaning only whole words match.

If you want to test this, you can replace "//surname" with strings like "Tay" and "Taylor".

Answer 130

Test version (with "York"):

```
contains("#New
York#Boston#Philadelphia#",concat("#","York","#"))
```

Full version (with "//city"):

```
contains("#New
York#Boston#Philadelphia#",concat("#",//city,"#"))
```

As the strings being matched can contain spaces, we need to use another character to separate items in the list. In this case, we used "#", but we could use any character that won't be found in a city name.

Answer 131

```
string-length(//postcode)
```

Answer 132

If you run:

```
//contact/node()
```

You will see that there are five nodes, two elements and three text nodes. The string-value includes the text of all of them. This means that the function counts the characters in all five nodes, including whitespace characters.

Answer 133

//customer//*[string-length() < 2]

Answer 134

string-length(translate(//postcode," ","")) <= 7

Answer 135

string(//li[.="red kangaroos"]/following-sibling::*[1])

Answer 136

string(//li[.="koala bears"]/preceding-sibling::*[1])

Answer 137

string(//li[.="koala bears"]/preceding-sibling::*[last()])

The XPath above works in this case, but it would fail if "koala bears" was the first animal in the list. A safer option would be:

string(//li[.="koala bears"]/../*)

This gets all the child elements of the same parent, and the string function takes the first of those by default. You can test it by replacing "koala bears" with "kangaroos". It still works.

//*[@id="article"]/descendant::p[1]

You might think you could do this:

//*[@id="article"]//p[1]

This doesn't work because "//" is shorthand for:

/descendant-or-self::node()/

Longhand, it reads:

//*[@id="article"]/descendant-or-self::node()/p[1]

If you leave off the "[1]" from each XPath you do get all the same descendants. However, with "//" you don't get them via the descendant axis. They are now each on the default child axes from their own parent nodes.

That's why you get three nodes from the XPath. They are three paragraphs which are the first children of their own parents.

//*[@id="article"]/descendant-or-self::div

Run:

//*[@id="article"]//div

This returns only the descendants. You can't use the "//" shorthand in this case either. At least, not as shown above.

Answer 140

//*[@id="article"]//self::div

This gets all the nodes and with less typing. They will each be on the self axis, but you get the same nodes.

Answer 141

//li[contains(.,"red")]/ancestor::div/h2

Note

You might notice that these two headers are returned in document order. You might also wonder why, as the ancestor axis should return their "div" nodes in reverse document order.

The ancestor axis does return nodes in reverse document order, but the two nodes are not on the ancestor axis of the same node. The list items are accessed in document order, and the ancestor axis followed for each of them, one after the other. Node order reversal happens within context, not to the overall results. In this case, with one node returned from each context, overall order stays the same.

Answer 142

//li[contains(.,"red") and ancestor::div[contains(h2,"Asia")]]

Answer 143

count(//book//keyword)

Answer 144

Neither.

The XPath will only match nodes in the document's default namespace. The "xmlns=" used in the examples sets the default namespaces of the rocket nodes: one to "spacex", the other to "fireworks". Therefore, the rocket nodes aren't in the default namespace any more.

No.

Elements without their own namespace node inherit the default namespace from their nearest namespaced ancestor. Therefore, the namespace of the colour node is also "fireworks".

Only "pyrotechnics".

The default namespace of the nearest ancestor replaces any other default namespace that could apply. More correctly, the default namespace set on the nearest ancestor-or-self node replaces any other default namespace: "effects" is in the "pyrotechnics" namespace too.

The "material" node for rocket-casing has a prefix, so it shares the namespace defined in its ancestor: "fireworks". The same applies to the node for "space paint": its namespace is "space". The other four materials have no prefixes, so the namespaces do not apply to them.

Perhaps that's because their use is not restricted to one specific industry. Regardless, prefixes defined in a node provide a way to apply namespaces to that node and its descendants, selectively.

166

By contrast, a default namespace is applied to the node it is defined in, and its descendants, automatically.

Answer 148

//*[@product_id=34]

Answer 149

namespace-uri(//*[@product_id=34])

Answer 150

//@product_id[.=34]

Answer 151

namespace-uri(//@product_id[.=34])

This returns "" i.e. an empty string. The ID attribute isn't prefixed, so doesn't share its element's namespace.

Answer 152

No.

You might try:

//@product_size[.="small"]

However, it doesn't work.

The product ID attribute isn't prefixed, so it isn't namespaced. The XPath returns it as normal.

The product size attribute is prefixed, so it is namespaced. The XPath doesn't return it: name-based node tests, like "product_size", don't match namespaced nodes.

Answer 153

//products/*[local-name() = "rocket"]

OR

//*[local-name()="rocket"]

Answer 154

//@*[local-name()="product_size"]

Answer 155

//*[@*[local-name()="product_size"]="small"]

Answer 156

namespace-uri(//*[@*[local-name()="product_size"]="small"])

Answer 157

//*[local-name() = "material" and namespace-uri() = "github.com/author-d-armstrong/xpath/fireworks"]

Answer 158

//*[local-name() = "material" and namespace-uri() != "github.com/author-d-armstrong/xpath/fireworks"]

Answer 159

//*[local-name() = "material" and namespace-uri() != namespace-uri(//products)]

The products node is in the document's default namespace, so this XPath gets nodes with namespaces that don't match the default.

Answer 160

//material

Answer 161

//*[name() = "s:material"]

Answer 162

//*[starts-with(name(),"s:")]

However, using the name function like this isn't always an option, because namespaces don't always come with prefixes.

Sometimes, the XML resets the default namespaces...

Answer 163

//*[namespace-uri() = "github.com/author-d-armstrong/xpath/space"]

Answer 164

//material

There are none. All the material elements are namespaced.

//@product_id

They all show up without specifying the namespace in the XPath, so they don't share that namespace.

If you want to confirm this, run:

namespace-uri(//@product_id[1])

They are attributes of their element node, not its descendants: their namespace is unaffected.

No answer 166 - not a problem-solving exercise

170

Notes

Notes

Notes

Notes

Notes

Notes